the glory of Kings

the glory of Kings

Tim Nordin

Cover and interior design by birdfoot.

Typeset in Berling Roman.

Software used to produce this book: Microsoft Windows; OpenOffice; NoteTab Light; Adobe InDesign; CorelDraw; Corel Photo-Paint; Adobe Acrobat; Animation Master

ISBN 978-0-9866662-0-9

Published by
birdfoot
PO Box 200
Amisk, AB
T0B 0B0
Canada

Version 1.0.0

REL006000
HRCG3

It is the glory of God to conceal a matter,
And the glory of kings to search a Matter out.

contents

introduction

what love has taught me

I haven't been married for many years, but during those years one thing has become clear. The most important lesson in the process of love is learning to love someone for who they are — not who you wish them to be, hope they are, or believe they can be. Love only exists in a willingness to face truth. Christ, as our example, died for us while we were yet sinners.[1] God's love was demonstrated in the face of truth. Likewise, a true love for God only exists in a place where we are willing to face the truth of who he is — not who we wish him to be, hope he is, or believe he can be.

Jesus assured us that there was a time coming when he would no longer speak to us in riddles, but would tell us plainly of the Father.[2] This was both a promise

1 Romans 5:8
2 John 16:25

and a threat, for through understanding comes sight, and through sight comes judgment. The warning that,"no man can see the face of God and live,"[3] is true to this day. There is a price to pay for this plain speech. Yet seek it we do, even though it will, in the words of Isaiah, cause us to come undone.[4] But where do we begin?

Many areas of study begin with the logic of first principles. These are the underlying structure, the framework into which the body of knowledge will fit. This book purposes to start a process of revealing the first principles of God. The Spirit willing, we are going to begin looking beyond the riddles and into the unseen.

Fractal is a term coined by Benoit Mandelbrot to describe a form of geometry he devised. It is a play on the Latin fractus, and loosely means *irregular fragments*. Many of these forms are recursive; that is, they are identical at any scale.[5] Think of a tree. A tree looks like a branch, which looks like a twig, which looks like the veining on a leaf. There is a similarity of pattern all the way up and down.

The prophetic word is very much a living recursive fractal. That word does not go out, accomplish a thing and then die. Rather, that word defines a pattern, and events that pertain to the theme of that word will follow the pattern delineated by that word. This is the reason that there is a lot of argumentation over certain scriptures and whether or not they have been fulfilled. You will be able to look at the history of creation at any magnification and find the pattern of that prophetic word and events that fit that pattern.

It is somewhat like a scale in western music. Imagine the piano keys as the flow of history. You can start at any key and play a major scale. The number of sharps and flats in that scale will differ. The number of white keys vs. black keys played will change. But every major scale will follow

3 Exodus 33:20
4 Isaiah 6:5
5 Benoit B. Mandelbrot, *The Fractal Geometry of Nature*, WH Freeman and Company, 1977, 1983.

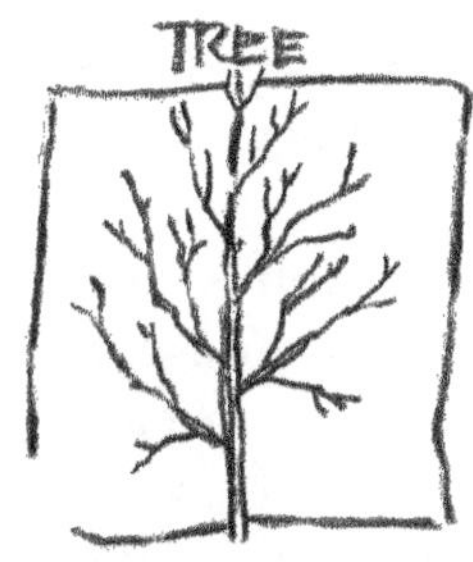

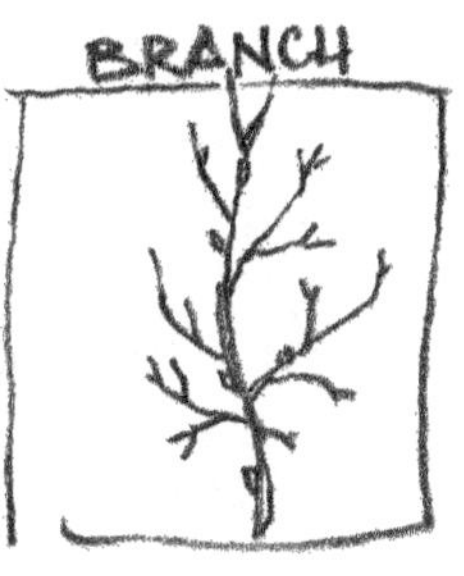

the pattern of step, step, half step, step, step, step, half step.

Every individual is also a collection of patterns. An understanding and recognition of these patterns allows you to identify and know someone. Our features, our speech, our moods, reactions to specific inputs, clothing choices, how we style (or neglect to style) our hair, are all bits and pieces of who we are and what makes it possible for people to relate to us. If you know a person well, you will recognize them at a distance walking away from you.

The same is true of God. The better you know his patterns, the easier it will be for you to recognize him. It is just a matter of how deep you want to go. We tend to be pretty flippant about saying we want to see Jesus. Isaiah tells us that Christ has no form or majesty, and when we see him, there is no beauty that we should desire him.[6] Let us accept that the problem isn't in sight, the problem is in recognition.

I will tell you a parable. There was a woman who's husband went on a journey into a far and distant land. Many evenings that woman would sit by the fire, and, filled with the memories of the place in which she sat, would feel very close to her husband, though he was half a world away. One day she received word that her husband desired her to come to the place in which he was labouring. And so she set off. The journey was very long, over mountains, upon oceans, through deserts and hostile lands. So it happened that, after the difficulties she endured and now among strange

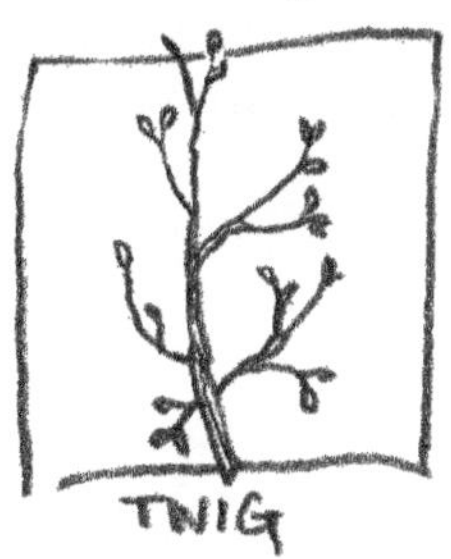

6 Isaiah 53:2

and unfamiliar surroundings, her husband seemed worlds distant, even though she was at last only minutes away from seeing him again.

The point is this: your feelings about where God is, and his actual location, have very little in common. You can feel God is near when all you are doing is living in past experience. You can also feel God is half a world away, when your journey has brought you closer than you have ever been. If you want to push into deeper understanding, there are going to be many times you feel as if you have lost your anchor, when it is just that you have been given more chain.

Think of God like a circle. When you look at a circle, that circle en-scribes and describes a transcendental. Now, you can look at circles all your life without recognizing that you are seeing the infinite. On the other hand, you can learn some basics, and come to the understanding that the ratio of the circumference of a circle to its diameter is a number we denote by the Greek letter π (pi), and that pi is a number that can never be fully calculated, because its decimal portion goes on forever.

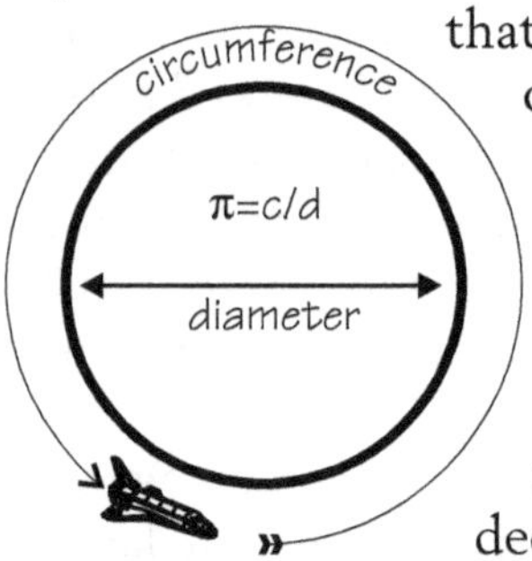

If you want to traverse a circle, it is necessary to use the finite to describe the infinite. A man with a degree of understanding will use 3.14 to represent pi. A bit more mathematically inclined person may go so far as 3.14159. The calculator in Microsoft's Windows XP uses an impressive 3.14159265358979323846264338327 95.

I've read that pi to the 39th decimal point will calculate the circumference of the known universe to within less than ¼ inch.[7] Of what use are more digits than this? Yet it keeps going. With the use of computers, pi has now been calculated to billions of digits, and there is still no end

7 Jonathan Borwein, Peter Borwein, "Ramanujan and Pi," *Pi: A Source Book*, Springer Verlag, 1997. p. 588.

in sight. Because it is infinite, regardless of how far you journey, you are only just starting.

Most of us, in our God journey, find a place where we really don't see the need for any more of God than what we already have. He has calculated our universe to within less than ¼ inch. Yet he keeps going. And we have only just begun. It is our universe that is too small. It is time to allow our boundaries to expand, and press in to know the Lord.

In his prologue to *The Lord of the Rings,* J.R.R. Tolkien describes Hobbits this way, "… they liked to have books filled with things that they already knew, set out fair and square with no contradictions." A grand description of the state of denominations. There is a very human tendency to wrap ourselves in an armour of doctrine, with the result that that which was meant to protect from heresy becomes protection for heresy. We begin to follow letter — not Spirit — and death enters.

Solomon was the wisest man who will ever live.[9] That wisdom allowed him to see well beyond his own time, and one thing he saw was the state of the church in this day. He described it as a period of the simple, the scoffer and the fool.[10] The *fool,* in some way, denies Christ — he wasn't the preexistent son of God, or, he didn't really die on the cross, or, he was only resurrected in spirit, not in body. The *scoffer* denies the Spirit — the age of miracles passed with the apostles, or, there is no need for a special presence of the Spirit upon you as he comes in at salvation, or, the whole tongues thing is silly. The *simple* deny the Father — God is beyond our understanding so just be content, or, debate is antithetical to unity, or, God said it, I believe it, that settles it. Every sect and denomination will generally fall into one of these categories. When it comes to a triune God, moving beyond the theoretical is something few have managed to accomplish.

8 JRR Tolkien, *The Lord of the Rings,* Houghton Mifflin Company, p. 7.
9 1 Kings 3:12
10 Proverbs 1:22

Language itself speaks of our lack of spiritual awareness. Language coalesces around those things we recognize, utilize and value. The more substance a thing has in our lives, the more terms and phrases we have to describe said thing. We have plenty of words for things both physical and mental. Certain concepts, such as money, have tens, if not hundreds, of descriptors. But when it comes to the spiritual, how do we fare? There are probably not even tens of words for the whole spiritual realm. And even those words that speak of the spiritual are not understood as such. For example, the word *revelation* becomes a term used to describe a mental happening, not a spiritual one.

In his novel *Babel-17,* Samuel Delany writes of an intergalactic war in which victory lies in a form of communication, a language that is closer to spiritual language than any form currently on earth. In one passage, the poetess heroine, Rydra Wong, lies in her room contemplating language. She is thinking about the room being blue and round and warm and smooth. She considers that the French language has no word for warm, only hot and tepid, and asks herself the question, "If there's no word for it, how do you think about it? And, if there isn't the proper form, you don't have the how, even if you have the words."[11] If you don't think it, you don't have the language for it, and if you don't have the language for it, you don't think it. Thus we are prevented from entering spiritual realms, for how does one speak that which is not as though it were[12] when the thought of it does not occur? Paul tells of being in paradise, and of the unspeakable words which it is not possible for a man to utter.[13]

Slowly we begin to grasp the extent of the restraint put upon men at the tower of Babel. The confusion of language has hidden the spiritual. It is only when this truth comes to light, when we are taught to express the inexpressible,

11 Samuel R. Delany, *Babel-17,* Ace Books, Sixth Printing 1978, Part Three, Chapter I, p. 125.

12 Romans 4:17

13 2 Corinthians 12:4

that the spiritual will take its place with the physical and mental in our lives.

There is an old story from India of a group of blind men who stumble upon an elephant. It is wonderfully retold in English verse by John Godfrey Saxe. Each man grabs part of the elephant, one man an ear, one man a leg, one man the tail, etc. And the description each man has of the elephant is based on the part of the elephant he is touching. Thus, the man holding the tail says, "An elephant is like a rope!" That is our experience with God. Each of us touch him in a certain way, but that touch becomes an absolute descriptor of who he is. So when we hear that, "God is bigger than we can imagine," what occurs to us is, "Ohhh! God is a really long rope!" To extrapolate outside and beyond our own experience is, perhaps, impossible, so what we need is a new experience, a new journey.

Jeremiah tells us that God's mercies are new every morning.[14] We have interpreted this to mean fresh. Like manna, it's the same loaf, just not stale. This is like using pi equals 3.14 for every calculation. We are introduced to a greater meaning in the first chapter of Genesis. Each day brought something new; something that hadn't been seen before; something new to come to understand; something new to add greater meaning to what had come previously.

If we just want to examine ideas that lie upon our own threshold we can be taken aback. For example, we are told that, "In the beginning was the word, and this word was with God, and this word was God."[15] This is no mere anthropomorphic view of scripture, but defines a word that is living and active.[16] Passages such as, "your word have I hidden in my heart that I might not sin against you,"[17] and "be one who does the word, not only a hearer of that word,"[18] show us the link between the written and

14 Lamentations 3:22 - 23
15 John 1:1
16 Hebrews 4:12
17 Psalm 119:11
18 James 1:22

the active word. Paul goes so far as to show the life of the word through phraseology such as, "the scripture, having foreseen that God would justify the Gentiles through faith, preached the gospel to Abraham."[19]

Many, including myself, have accepted this bond between the person of Christ and the active word of God; however, this has some very interesting implications. Given the preexistence of the word, did God predestine man, or did man define God? To elaborate, consider that the word is full of the stories of men. If Christ is that word, and that word existed before creation, did the preexistence of that word predestine Noah, Abraham, David, et alii, or did the actions of those men define Christ? We don't like either avenue. And it didn't take much digging to arrive at this question. If your theology isn't robust enough to give you a door into understanding, you need a more robust theology.

Many speak of a harvest in the last days.[20] It is also referred to by many as a harvest of souls. This is, perhaps, an incomplete thought. Consider the parable of the sower.[21] Sowing and germination appear to be the time of salvation. If you have worked on the farm at all, you will know that harvest speaks of maturity. It is only when that sown and germinated seed has grown and begins to ripen that harvest begins.

Amos speaks of a time when the plowman will overtake the harvester.[22] I have only heard this spoken of as a blessing, but to a farmer it looks more like a curse. What happens when the fieldwork passes the combine? The harvest is plowed under. Why would this be done? Because the grain has not come to maturity, it has produced no fruit, therefore it will be plowed under to fertilize the next crop.

John the Baptist warns about this when he states that the axe is already at the root of the tree, and those that fail

19 Galatians 3:8
20 Revelation 14:15
21 Matthew 13:3-9
22 Amos 9:13

to produce good fruit will be cut down and thrown into the fire.[23] That ash fertilizes the trees that are producing. In John's time this was a word to the Israelites, to those who had been entrusted with the things of God. History tells us the result. Who was fertilized with that ash and entrusted with the things of God? Who are the words of Amos meant for, and what will be the result in our age?

The time for maturity is upon us. And, too, the danger of falling away.[24] Just as a runner will fall away from the pack if her training is insufficient, so will the called of this age risk falling away if they are unprepared to recognize the Lord. So let us press in. Let us determine if there really is a foundation of first principles in the word that can prepare us to see God.

I have taken a somewhat heuristic approach in the preparation of the following material. There are two reasons for this. The first is that I don't have all the answers. The second is that I am not going to reveal every answer I possess. The need is for you to press in. My hope is that you are provoked to do just that.

23 Matthew 3:10
24 2 Thessalonians 2:3

1 one

in the beginning

The word *list* has a number of different meanings in English. The one that concerns us here is the most common meaning, though I would ask you to, "list while I speak of lists" — in a hearing and not a fainting fashion.

List is both a verb and a noun, with the action producing the object. If you list, you end up with a list. Lists have the power to organize objects and actions. When you write a list, the action organizes objects, and when you follow a list, the objects organize your actions. I am a list person, but the problem is that I only like to write them, not follow them. When the impulse strikes, it is common to see me jotting down a list, but it is admittedly a lot rarer to see me putting that list into application. I guess that makes me half a list person. God is not a half a list person. He both arranges and acts.

The power of lists is seen in the fact that God's word begins with one. There have been countless arguments and debates over the centuries about the list that begins the book of Genesis. The problem with these arguments is that they never define the list. Without definition, a list can take on any meaning you wish. It is possible to argue on this arbitrary footing, but not very profitable.

For example, suppose I hand you a piece of paper on which is scrawled the following:

tomato
apple
artichoke
celery
rutabaga

You can apply a variety of meanings to this list. Perhaps it is a shopping list, the things I should pick up at the grocery store on my way home from work. Perhaps it is a list of foods to which I am allergic and that you should avoid serving me if you don't want to see me inflate like a balloon. Perhaps they are choices for a side dish at that new home-style restaurant down the street or seeds I am going to purchase and plant in my garden. It is only when you are told that these are the potential names for my new kitten that the list takes on its true meaning in your mind. In like manner, the list that begins Genesis only takes on its true meaning when given the correct heading.

After that introduction, you may be surprised to find out that we are not searching for this heading. Rather, we are stepping back and looking at a broader picture, and what we see is eye opening. We discover that this list is itself a heading. This list defines the scriptures — it is the *pattern of revelation.*

Possibly you have read that the number seven speaks of completion, but a more exact term would be finished revelation. Revelation walks through to its completion in seven steps. These seven steps are thoroughly detailed in the scriptures, and the first place we encounter them is, very appropriately, in the beginning. Let us look at this list a bit closer and see if we can find some additional information.

These seven steps are the process that has gained the title *The Six Days of Creation* because, though each has been demarked by the term *day,* the first six show God doing some heavy lifting. The last day is associated with doing nothing and so apparently doesn't count. This is unfortunate, because the seventh day is the culmination of the process of the previous six.

If we start with the first verse of the first chapter of Genesis, we will, in the space of thirty-five verses, walk through the happenings of each day. A fairly cursory reading will show that these seven days can be quickly split into two divisions:

6
1st day of creating
2nd day of creating
3rd day of creating
4th day of creating
5th day of creating
6th day of creating

1
7th day, a day of rest

This is our first theme. Any process of revelation is divisible into this pattern of six and one. If it cannot be divided in this way, it isn't true revelation. These divisions are not always immediately apparent, though many are, yet this is the face of revelation, and all real revelation will show this face, this *pattern of revelation.*

God's revelation of his character to Moses reiterates this pattern, "You shall work six days, but the seventh day you shall rest."[1] God was making the Israelites a people of his own possession,[2] and so those people needed to conform to his character and take on his traits. He tells the Israelites, "This is me, this is my pattern, and you must conform to that pattern in order to come to an understanding of who I am."

1 Exodus 20:9-10
2 Deuteronomy 14:2

The self-help guru Tony Robbins demonstrates a process he calls *matching and mirroring.* Tony will bring two people onto the stage. He has the first person think of an event in their life, then asks them to duplicate the way their body was acting at that time. He then has the second person match the the first person's posture, their facial expression, the way they are standing and breathing. The second person suddenly has insight into what the first person is feeling and often even knows what they were thinking and doing — their thoughts and emotions begin mirroring those of the person they are matching.[3] A matching of the physical produces a mirroring of the mental. This is why we are instructed to walk as Christ walked,[4] and to have the same mind as Christ.[5] This isn't so that we merely become little Jesus clones. Our matching of the physical and the mental produces a mirroring of the spiritual.

God's revelation of promise to the Israelites when they entered Canaan is shown in the taking of the city of Jericho.[6] The Israelites are instructed to march around the city once every day for six days, carrying the ark of the Lord, while seven priests blow seven trumpets continually. On the seventh day, they were told to march around the city seven times, then to shout. When they followed these instructions, the wall protecting the city fell down, and the city was captured. We can see here that the seventh day is the fulfillment of the actions of the first six days, just as the *rest* of God is the fulfillment of the actions of creation.

The heavens declare the glory of God and the firmament is proclaiming the work of his hands.[7] Since creation, his invisible character, eternal power and divine nature have been clearly seen and understood through what he has

3 Anthony Robbins, *Unlimited Power*, Fawcett Columbine, Ballantine Edition, 1987, p. 161.
4 1 John 2:6
5 Philippians 2:5
6 Joshua 6
7 Psalms 19:1

made.[8] The theme of creation is the revealing of God. He is revealing himself both to creation and through creation. If that is true, we can then hypothesize that biblical history, the history of the revelation of God to man, will divide into seven steps in the manner of the seven days of creation, in accordance with this *pattern of revelation*.

Biblical history places the transgression of Adam at approximately 4000 BC. It is at this breaking of the commandment that the process begins, for man now had the knowledge of good and evil and could comprehend what he was being taught. The journey from that time until now has been about 6000 years. Peter, extrapolating upon Psalm 90, tells us that with the Lord a day is like

a thousand years, and a thousand years are as a day.[9] The implication of this is apparent in our current discussion. We can divide these 6000 years into six steps of 1000 years each. Does this fit our pattern?

6
- 1st thousand years
- 2nd thousand years
- 3rd thousand years
- 4th thousand years
- 5th thousand years
- 6th thousand years

So far so good. To complete this *pattern of revelation* we only need to extrapolate a bit.

6 Six thousand years of history
1 7th thousand years

8 Romans 1:20
9 2 Peter 3:8

This theme begins to conform to a non-amillennial view, aligning the restoration of the kingdom[10] with a thousand year reign of Christ.[11] If that is so, we would complete our pattern as follows:

6 Six thousand years of history

1 One thousand year reign of Jesus Christ

Compelling, but far from sealing the deal; however, this isn't the only instance of the *pattern of revelation* in the scriptures. Let us take a brief tour and see what other evidence we can unearth.

10 Acts 1:6
11 Revelation 20:4

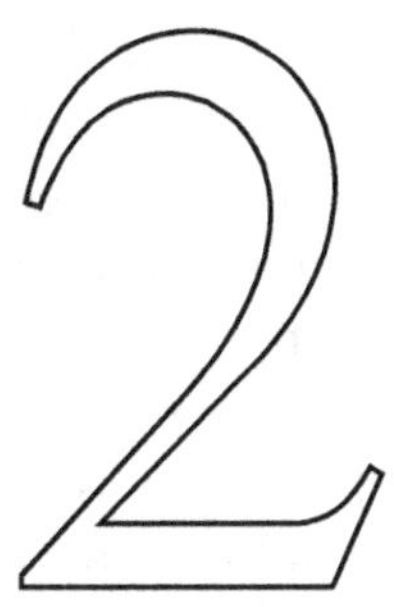

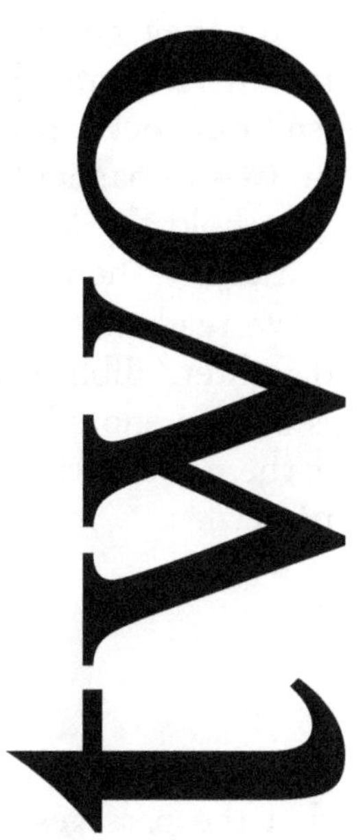

the doe-eyed maiden

When it comes to favourite biblical characters, you won't find Leah topping too many lists. Lately, though, I have begun to regard her in a new light. We really don't know how complicit she was in her father Laban's plot to ensnare the services of Jacob, but then neither was Rachel all that ready to spill the beans. Surely Rachel wasn't completely ignorant of what was happening. Yet it was Leah that was put into that most thankless place, a pawn of her family, unloved by her husband.

Perhaps one of the saddest verses in the scriptures is, "And when the Lord saw that Leah was hated, he opened her womb; but Rachel was barren."[1] Jacob's hatred brought blessing, and his love brought a curse, yet he could hardly be held culpable for his awkward family. It wasn't circumstances that brought them to that place, but the pattern of God. Jacob's life weaves the grand design of the Spirit of God, and because of that, his is a story that holds deep revelation.

1 Genesis 29:31

You may be thinking that the seven years of Jacob's labour falls into this pattern. I imagine it does, but that isn't our focus. It is with Leah that we concern ourselves now — in particular, Leah's blessing. It is Leah's children who hold the key to unlocking the greatest mysteries of our age — the times and seasons.

We read that Leah had six sons and afterwards bore a daughter.[2] Biblically, the mention of the birth of a daughter is always enough to pique one's attention. In this case it is the punctuation needed to conform her children to the pattern.

6 Six sons
1 One daughter

If we examine the text a bit closer, though, we see that the passages recording the births of Leah's children don't run concurrently. A more complex theme begins to emerge.[3]

Four sons

she ceases bearing
children for a time

Two sons and one daughter

The birth of her daughter is mentioned immediately following the birth of her last two sons. There is a link between the three, and we could write down the children's births as:

4 Four births
3 Three births

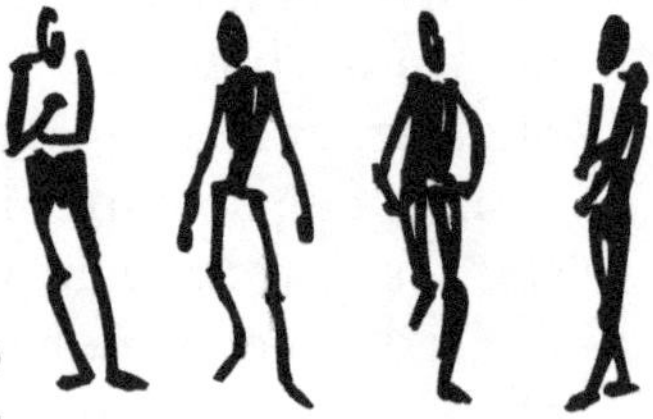

However, it would be foolish to ignore the change in gender. Boys and girls are not the same, and as the French would say,

2 Genesis 30:20-21
3 Genesis 29:31-35

"Vive la différence!" A better arrangement would make note of this fact.

4	1st birth, a son 2nd birth, a son 3rd birth, a son 4th birth, a son
2	5th birth, a son 6th birth, a son
1	7th birth, a daughter

It is important to keep in mind that there is a tie between the Two Steps and the One Step, a story that binds them together.

The pattern is the pattern. What holds for one holds for all. Subsequently, we can begin to check our work. Let's glance back at Genesis and the days of creation. Can we find this 4:2:1 *pattern of revelation*? Even a quick read will reveal:

4	Forming habitation, days 1-4
2	Forming inhabitants, days 5 & 6
1	Day of rest, day 7

During the first four days, the place of habitation, both a space to live in and food to eat, are formed. Then, during the next two days, inhabitants to live in the space and to consume the food are formed. Finally, on the last day, the creator rests (the culmination is *rest*).

How about history? Does this *pattern of revelation* hold there? From Adam's transgression to the life of Jesus Christ on earth the bible records 4000 years. Jesus established the church, and that church has now been in existence for 2000 years. If we are, at this time, moving into a millennial kingdom, then the pattern holds.

4	1st thousand years	Adam to Noah
	2nd thousand years	Noah to Abraham
	3rd thousand years	Abraham to David
	4th thousand years	David to Christ
2	5th thousand years	Church
	6th thousand years	Church
1	7th thousand years	Millennial reign

We can then surmise that there is a link between the forming of the inhabitants of the earth and the day of rest of which we were previously unaware. Likewise, there is a similar link between the church age and the millennial reign.

It isn't just the further confirmation of our growing pattern that is exciting. There is more information to be gleaned. Each of the children have a name, that name has a meaning, and that meaning can be applied to the appropriate section of the pattern. For example, the first son's name is Reuben. The name Reuben means, "See, A Son." This, then, is the theme of the first day of creation. And the first thousand years of history.

4	Reuben	See, a Son	Adam to Noah
	Simeon	One who hears	Noah to Abraham
	Levi	Attached	Abraham to David
	Judah	Praise	David to Christ
2	Issachar	Reward	Church
	Zebulun	Honour	Church
1	Dinah	Justice	Millennial reign

Each iteration of the pattern gives up more information. Each piece of information applies to every iteration of the pattern. So, the structure grows in its fractal-like way with each new piece both taking and giving so that we might better understand.

Each of those children also had and have a destiny, a role to fill and fulfill. The destiny of each child speaks to both the individual and to the pattern as a whole. Can we find an example? One excellent place to start is the prophetic words of Jacob and Moses upon the tribes of Israel. Let us look at an easy example — the words of Jacob to Judah.[4] In the span of history, Judah speaks of the period of time from the enthronement of David until the coming of Jesus Christ. Jacob's words to Judah also speak of this time, when Judah — and David was of the tribe of Judah — would receive kingship over the people, and that kingship would pass down though David's household for one thousand years until the Messiah came from out of this household and took kingship forever.

One theme of Jacob's word to Judah is governance. With that in mind, take the same words of Jacob and apply them to the fourth day of creation.[5] One scripture that parallels this thought is Balaam's prophecy that a star will come out of Jacob,[6] which speaks of the coming of the Messiah. This may not be the only path. Another idea that occurs is the establishment of principalities and powers, those who "rule the day and the night." With this hypothesis in hand one can ask questions like, "Why would God covenant with the day and the night?"[7] and, "What does it mean that the night is far past and the day almost here?"[8]

And Dinah, as a daughter, has no words spoken over her (silence). What does that tell us about the next thousand years?

4 Genesis 49:9-12
5 Genesis 1:14-19
6 Numbers 24:17
7 Jeremiah 33:20
8 Romans 13:12

Jesus tells us that the Kingdom of Heaven belongs to those who are like children.[9] I believe part of that is a willingness to be instructed. Children come prepared to learn, not to bend learning to their own conceptualization. This is why we are directed not to lean into our own understanding,[10] and it is why learning for an adult is fraught with problems. We want to twist everything new into our own imperfect pattern. Rather, we must learn God's pattern, then examine our own beliefs to find out whether or not they fit.

Well, we have seen enough of the *pattern of revelation* that we are now going to throw something new into the mix, and that new thing comes from the Book of Daniel.

9 Matthew 19:14
10 Proverbs 3:5

the center of all things

The Book of Daniel introduces us to, appropriately enough, a man named Daniel. This man is described as one who served his God continually[1] and was given wisdom and power by that same God.[2] Daniel tells us that his God reveals deep and hidden things.[3] So, if a man with God's wisdom and power says that same God will reveal secrets to us, then examining the book he wrote has awesome potential for revelation.

The position of the center, or in the midst, has always been one of significance, so our languages and cultures are replete with examples. "All roads lead to Rome," speaks of Rome being the hub, the center, the place of greatest importance. "Caught between Scylla and Charybdis," identifies the center as the place of greatest difficulty and trial. Goldilocks and the Three Bears associates the center

1 Daniel 6:20
2 Daniel 2:23
3 Daniel 2:22

as the place of greatest pleasure or satisfaction, "Not too hot, not too cold, but just right." Genesis records a tree of decision occupying the center of the garden of Eden.[4]

Daniel lived at the center of history. It had been 3500 years since Adam's transgression, and the end of the millennial period was 3500 years in the future. And it is through the book of Daniel that we can begin to learn what the center means.

Israel had been overrun by the Babylonians and their king, Nebuchadnezzar, had deported the people to his own country. Nebuchadnezzar became the king of Babylon in 605 BC and under his reign the city of Babylon became "one of the most magnificent cities of the ancient world."[5] The Hanging Gardens in Babylon are called one of the seven wonders of the ancient world.

During this period of time the Greeks were tottering on their first steps toward democracy and would soon give rise to the likes of Socrates and Plato. In China, the Chou dynasty ruled, and the philosopher Confucius was born. India was birthing a new religion under the teachings of Siddhartha, who came to be known as Buddha (Buddha, interestingly, means *enlightened*). The Persians were plotting to overthrow the Medes and would, under the leadership of Cyrus, capture Babylon, then on to the Thermopylae (Pass of the Hot Springs) of graphic novel and movie fame.

At this center, though, the focus is Babylon. And within Babylon, Nebuchadnezzar.

Nebuchadnezzar was described by God as one who had lordship over nature and a dominion which extended to the far parts of the earth; a position in which God had placed him.[6] Through a dream which Daniel interprets, God warns him that he is going to be removed from his position, and that seven times are going to pass by until, when he attests to the sovereignty of heaven, his

4 Genesis 3:3

5 Finkelstein, Jacob J, "Nebuchadnezzar," *World Book Encyclopedia*, 1979 edition.

6 Daniel 4:20-22

kingdom will be assured. Lo and behold, a year later, while Nebuchadnezzar is walking in the most magnificent garden on the earth, the dream comes to pass.[7]

Now this sounds familiar. We know someone else who is spoken of as being put on a path of lordship over nature and dominion over the earth. He was given the word that the day he ate of the tree he would be removed from his position. Lo and behold, while walking in the most magnificent garden on the earth, the word comes to pass. That man was Adam, and it was decreed for Adam that seven times, or seven thousand years, would pass until, when he attests to the sovereignty of heaven, his kingdom will be assured.

The center is a snapshot, a revisiting of the events at the beginning. The center brings wisdom that the beginning might be understood, and with that understanding comes power.

This enhances our *pattern of revelation*. We now have:

4	1st 2nd 3rd 4th - the center
2	5th 6th
1	7th

The fourth step occupies the place of the center, therefore the fourth step should demonstrate and elaborate upon the first. Let us revisit our former examples and see if this holds true.

First, let us look at the days of creation. The first day is described as:

A day light is brought into being

A day in which light and dark were separated and named[8]

7 Daniel 4:28 - 33
8 Genesis 1:1 - 5

The fourth day is described as:

> A day lights are brought into being
>
> A day in which day and night are separated
>
> A day in which the light will bring knowledge — the lights are for signs and seasons and days and years[9]

The fourth day both demonstrates and elaborates upon the first.

How about the sons of Leah? The first son was Reuben, the fourth son was Judah. As was previously mentioned, the meaning of Reuben is, "See, A Son." Reuben was the first born and the inheritance was his right. With that inheritance came a double portion of wealth, the role of religious head and the place of ultimate authority over his household. His episode with his father's concubine barred him from the inheritance[10] and that inheritance was divided. Joseph received the double portion, through the entitlement of both of his sons, Ephraim and Manasseh.[11] Levi received the role of priest[12] and Judah the place of authority.[13] These remained divided until a man from Judah, from the line of Kings, was restored back to the place of the double portion,[14] of priesthood[15] and headship.[16] That man was Jesus Christ. So Judah, through Jesus Christ, both demonstrates and elaborates upon the theme of, "See, A Son."

The center shows off another aspect through a pattern that was given to

9 Genesis 1:14-19
10 Genesis 49:3-4
11 Genesis 48:9
12 Numbers 1:48-54
13 Genesis 49:10
14 Hebrews 1:2-4; Ephesians 1:17-23
15 Hebrews 7:15
16 Colossians 1:18

Daniel. Let us call this the *pattern of times*. Its format is, "Time, times and half a time."[17] Add this up on a basic level:

$$\text{Time} + \text{Times} + \tfrac{1}{2}\ \text{Time}$$
$$= 1 + 2 + \tfrac{1}{2}$$
$$= 3\ \tfrac{1}{2}$$

and the sum is 3 ½.

This can also be viewed in a different fashion. As an example, think of one dozen eggs. Are one dozen eggs, one or twelve? They are both. Twelve individual eggs are one group of twelve eggs. In like manner, let us imagine that time means two. This would mean times (time x 2) would equal four, and half a time (time x ½), would equal one. Now our equation looks as follows:

$$\text{Time} + \text{Times} + \tfrac{1}{2}\ \text{Time}$$
$$= 2 + 4 + 1$$
$$= 7$$

Now, where have we seen the elements 4, 2 & 1 before? In our *pattern of revelation*, of course. Correlating this new information with the days of creation, we find:

4	days of forming habitation	Times
2	days of forming inhabitants	Time
1	day of rest	Half a time

With the children of Leah, we find:

4	sons	Times
2	sons	Time
1	daughter	Half a Time

17 Daniel 12:7

With Biblical history, we find:

4000 years	Adam to Christ	Times
2000 years	Church History	Time
1000 years	Millennial Reign	Half a Time

Now, let us look back at the time of Daniel. In 500 years, Jesus Christ would come to the earth. A breakdown of the years is as follows:

BC 500 to 1	500 years	Daniel to Christ
AD 1 to 2000	2000 years	Church history
AD 2000-3000	1000 years	Millennial Reign

or

500 years	Daniel to Christ	Half a Time
2000 years	Church History	Times
1000 years	Millennial Reign	Time

We see the time, times, half a time *pattern of times* reiterated in Daniel's period in history, at the center. This is understandable, since we have stated that the center demonstrates the beginning. You can think of it as a piece of paper folded in half. The piece on each side of the fold is descriptive of the whole.

In the breakdown of 7000 years, the 4000 years encompassing the transgression and the law, from Adam to Christ, falls in the *times* category:

4000 years	Adam to Christ	Times
2000 years	Church History	Time
1000 years	Millennial Reign	Half a Time

In the breakdown of the last 3500 years, it is the period of church history that falls in the *times* category:

500 years	Daniel to Christ	Half a Time
2000 years	Church History	Times
1000 years	Millennial Reign	Time

From this foundation a framework can be built that aids our understanding of what it means to occupy the position of the center. We can also begin applying what we currently know to scripture.

One immediate application is found when Peter speaks of Christ, "appearing at the end of the times."[18] We see this is true in both examples of the *pattern of revelation* as it applies to Biblical history. Starting from the beginning he appeared at the end of 4000 years — after the years of the transgression and the law, or times, and starting from the center he will appear at the end of 2000 years — after the years of church history, also known as times.

Another point to consider is that "time, times, half a time," takes us toward or away from a center. Any grouping that falls into this pattern, in a fractal-like manner, ultimately shows off only half of the whole, just as in the example of the folded piece of paper. The time line of history parallels the *pattern of times* as follows:

4	4000-3000	Adam to Noah	Times
	3000-2000	Noah to Abraham	
	2000-1000	Abraham to David	
	1000-1 BC	David to Christ	
2	1 AD-1000	Church	Time
	1000-2000	Church	
1	2000-3000	Millennial Reign	Half a time

18 1 Peter 1:20

Because of this it is important to recognize that this is only half of a whole, only one side of a folded piece of paper. Where and what is the other half? Was it the period of time Adam was in the garden? Is it a time that is coming after the millennium? And what about the days of creation, and Leah's children, who also fit into this pattern? What are we being told there?

There are a lot of questions to be answered.

When the *pattern of times*, "time, times, half a time," is mentioned, probably the first book that comes to mind isn't the book of Daniel, but The Revelation, and it is to that book we will now turn our attention.

lifting the veil

The year is 95 AD. Jerusalem has been destroyed by Roman legionnaires under the command of the emperor Vespasian's son, Titus. Christians suffer waves of persecution. Eleven of the twelve disciples of Christ have been martyred. The twelfth, John, is living in exile on the island of Patmos. And it is there, at that place and that time, that he is given a revelation of what is to come. And not just your average revelation, but a revelation that was first given to Jesus Christ himself, in order to show his servants.[1]

If we understand seven as a culmination of revelation, then the book of Revelation should be a book of sevens, and so it is. The first chapter alone introduces us to:

Seven churches
Seven Spirits around the Throne
Seven golden lamp stands
Seven stars
Seven angels

1 Revelation 1:1

It also pays to be aware of alternate presentations of seven, those which conform to the *pattern of revelation*. For example, in that same first chapter we find the Godhead[2] described as:

4	Who is Who was Who is to come The seven Spirits around the Throne
2	Faithful witness Firstborn from the dead
1	Ruler of the Kings of the earth

All these tantalizing paths! Where does one start? Of all our choices, I think our best launch point is the seven Spirits.

Because there are seven Spirits, the first connection we can make is that the Spirit of God is intimately linked to the completeness of the revelation of God. This is the identity of the Spirit. When you look at the days of creation, or at Leah's children, you are looking at the Spirit of God. The pattern is the Spirit, and the information contained within the pattern is the mystery of God. When God commands Moses to make everything according to the pattern shown to him on the mountain,[3] he was speaking about the Spirit.

Connecting the Spirit to the pattern may be a difficult association to make. Think of a computer graphics file such as a jpeg. The data is bonded to the format and only viewable through the format. At the beginning of the file is a jpeg header that enables the jpeg data to be read correctly. Without the header, the information is merely a string of binary data, a bunch of 0s and 1s stuck in a row; however, viewed through the header, these 0s and 1s take form. The header isn't just adjunct to the whole, but is an intimate part. The data, viewed through the header — which is also part of the data — reveals a picture.

2 Revelation 1:4
3 Exodus 25:40

This explains the difficulty we have in recognizing God. The data is incomprehensible without the lens of the Spirit. Hagar named the Holy Spirit of God, "the God of seeing."[4] Thus we have the lamb with seven eyes which are the seven Spirits of God.[5] Without the Spirit of God continually adjusting our focus, we will miss much, both within the scriptures and without.

It is Isaiah who introduces us to the seven Spirits of God.[6] He is prophesying about the coming Messiah, and in this passage is saying that the completeness of the revelation of God is going to rest upon the anointed one. The seven are as follows:

The Spirit of the Lord
Wisdom
Understanding
Counsel
Might
Knowledge
Fear of the Lord

First, we must realize that this list is given in a descending order. How do we know that? We are told that the fear of the Lord is the beginning of wisdom, or that the fear of the Lord is the first step in the progression of revelation.[7] Let's reverse the list so it reads in the order we have been using:

Fear of the Lord
4 Knowledge
Might
Counsel

2 Understanding
Wisdom

1 The Spirit of the Lord

4 Genesis 16:13
5 Revelation 5:6
6 Isaiah 11:2
7 Proverbs 9:10

Again, this information is applicable to all iterations of the pattern, including those we have looked at thus far. So, what is shown off here is the aspect of the Spirit that has been at work during each thousand year period of history. Also, during each of the days of creation. And, it informs us that the millennial reign will be a time of the fullness of the Spirit.

The list of the seven Spirits is given in a particular grouping that would be foolish to ignore:

The Spirit of knowledge and fear of the Lord
The Spirit of counsel and might
The Spirit of wisdom and understanding
The Spirit of the Lord

This is a grouping we have not yet noticed. It runs:

We will leave this pattern alone for the time being and return to it in the next chapter.

One other salient point you will want to carry with you is that the term *the seven Spirits around the Throne* occurs in the center of the list of the Godhead:

4 Who is
Who was
Who is to come
The seven Spirits around the Throne

2 Faithful witness
Firstborn from the dead

1 Ruler of the Kings of the earth

As the center demonstrates and elaborates on the first, this tells us that these seven Spirits are also known as,

The God Who Is, and further investigation will prove this conjecture, but I leave that for your to-do list.

It is interesting that so many commentators see the events depicted in the book of Revelation as motivated or inspired by our adversary. We read about what Germany, Russia, China and Iran are doing. Why do we think it is the world who prepares the way of the Lord? Christ told us that there would be wars and rumours of wars, and that nation would rise up against nation.[8] But these are not the events that signal the return of Jesus Christ.

Two thousand years ago we could have been talking about the Babylonians, the Persians, the Greeks or the Romans; however, it wasn't any of these who were called out to prepare the way. Rather, one obscure man in the whole world, from a backwater country in the middle of a desert was anointed as the voice in the wilderness. If you heard that one voice, you knew the coming of the Messiah was at hand. As a Joseph, he was sent ahead.[9] Why do we think it would be any different in our day? Do not be surprised if the return of the Lord Jesus Christ begins with one man out of billions, in some backwater corner of the earth.

So, flipping ahead to chapter six, let us take a look at another example of the *pattern of revelation* — the seven seals. The seals easily divide into the *pattern of revelation*:

4 Four horsemen of the first four seals

2 Two seals of judgment; seals five & six

1 One seal of silence; the seventh seal

8 Matthew 24:6-7
9 Psalm 105:17

The first day of creation brings the implication of light, the speaking forth of the light, and the fourth day brings the fulfillment. The first son of Leah gives the promise of a son, the fourth son brings the fulfillment. The scriptures tell us that John the Baptist was not the light, he was not the son spoken of, but he came to bear witness of the light.[10] He was the implication of light, the promise of a son. And, in accordance with the pattern shown us, a witness to the return of the Lord will be raised up and will cry out in the wilderness. Those who are called and chosen will recognize that that voice has come, and will realize that the time of the first seal is upon them.

Do the opening of the seven seals align in some way to the great tribulation? The pattern is the pattern, and if there are seven years of tribulation, then there is definitely an alignment; however, the tribulation happens at a point during the time of the opening of the seals, so the actual fullness of the spirit of the seals isn't found merely in one seal per year of tribulation. Though we are not going to discuss the meaning of the seals, consider this: who you are in the beloved was sealed, became inaccessible, until the day of redemption, when the seal is opened.[11]

One point of interest before we carry on is that John, in his first epistle, tells us that this is the last hour.[12] That hour has been two thousand years long. We have seen that the seventh position in the *pattern of revelation* has a relationship with the millennium. So then, what might it mean when the seventh seal is opened and there is silence in heaven for half an hour?

Finally, before we move out of Revelation, let us take a look at the end. The twenty-first chapter gives us a brief description of the new heaven and new earth, and, because this is revelatory and it is about completion, naturally this description follows the *pattern of revelation*.

10 John 1:7-8
11 Ephesians 4:30
12 1 John 2:18

The tabernacle of God is among men
He will tabernacle with them
4 They will be his people
God himself will be with them and be
their God

He will wipe every tear from their eyes
2 Death, mourning, crying and pain will
be no more

1 For the first things have passed away

There are those who teach that Christ paid it all on the cross, the result of which is Utopia in our time. The problem is that to believe this we must ignore the fact that we have been called the body of Christ.[13] We are Christ on this earth.[14] And, while it is true that Christ paid it all, the purchase price is through his body, of which we are a part.

That is why the church age is identified in this passage as the time when he will wipe every tear from their eyes, and death, mourning, crying and pain will be no more. We are part of that process. Jesus suffered outside the city gate and we were called outside with him to bear his reproach.[15] There we remained for two thousand years. Paul tells us that his body completes the sufferings of Christ,[16] and so too the whole body — the church.

In our time, the body is called to Gilgal,[17] and that reproach is rolled away. Just as after two days the stone was rolled away and Christ came forth in the power of the resurrection, so, after two thousand years, the gates will be lifted up, the ancient doors opened[18] and those who have borne reproach outside the gates of the city will now enter in that power of the resurrection, having had

13 1 Corinthians 12:27
14 Galatians 2:20
15 Hebrews 13:12 - 13
16 Colossians 1:24
17 Joshua 5:9
18 Psalm 24:7 - 10

their reproach removed. Though it is the theme of the millennial period, even now the first things have begun to pass away. The iron and the clay become visible to those with the eyes to see.[19] This, the most difficult transition, has begun.

Next, let us take a look at foundation, which is seen by viewing the *pattern of revelation* through a different lens.

19 Daniel 2:42-43

the pillars of the earth

What comes to your mind when the topic swings to the establishment, or the foundation, of the heavens and the earth?

An uncle of mine tells a funny story about a contract he had to build a hall in a public park. The initial stages of construction are very much concerned with things that happen below your feet: the excavation of top soils; the establishment of a grade; the trucking in of the sand and gravel; and the compaction of the fill. Then there is the forming and pouring of the concrete slab upon which the frame will be constructed. Even the walls are assembled on the ground and then lifted into place.

Meanwhile, a local busybody had concerned herself with what was going on. She kept checking up on the job site, and, to her eyes, nothing was happening. There was nothing to see. One day, upset about what she perceived to be a lack of dedication, she went off on a mission. She picked up one of the park officials, complained to him about the lack of progress, then took him down to inspect the site. Naturally, that happened to be the day the walls were raised. When the inspectors arrived, there stood the framework for the entire building. It appeared that an awful lot of work had been done in one morning.

Just like the busybody, I believe the biggest mistake we make in speaking of creation is that we view it as an event and not a process. This is seen in headlines such as, *Creation vs. Evolution*. If someone says, *Apples vs. Oranges,* we have a fairly good idea of what is being discussed, but what is being said in *Creation vs. Evolution*? The underlying fabric is, *God vs. no God,* and, because evolution has been associated with process, by default creation — and our definition of God — becomes instantaneousness.

This is unfortunate, because it is our adversary who desires instantaneousness. Our God is a God of the type of immediacy that is found in the saying, "It took me seventeen years to become an overnight success." Conception happens in a moment, birthing happens in a moment, but the growth of the child takes time. Do not associate God, or creation, with only conception and birthing, but also with the growth that is a necessary part of complete development.

To understand what I am going to say, you have to understand that you are, right now, involved in the process of the creation of God. To state it more baldly, you are, right now, somewhere in the story of the days of creation. Creation is not some moment that happened at some point in the past, but it is the framework into which you are both being fitted and are fitting. You are not a bystander in the processes of God, but, as was shown by Adam,[1] you are a participant in creation.

The story of creation is one of prophetic revelation. To regard it as anything less is to make it mere fable. This is why the arguments for creation have devolved into sects, cults and the position of, as Richard Dawkins describes it, "Argument from Personal Incredulity."[2]

1 Genesis 2:19
2 Richard Dawkins, *The Blind Watchmaker*, WW Norton & Company, 1986, p. 38.

We are not going to take the time here to debate the merits of inflationary cosmology, but we are going to take a look at some basic thought about foundation. In doing so, we turn again to Solomon. Solomon laid out an interesting form of the *pattern of revelation* we have been discussing.[3] He tells us that Wisdom has:

4
Built her house
Hewn her seven pillars
Slaughtered her beasts
Mixed her wine

2
Set her table
Sent out her servant girls

1
Calls from the highest places in the town

Rather than deal with this pattern as a whole, note the second line, "Wisdom has hewn her seven pillars." These are the same pillars of which it is said, "The pillars of the earth are the Lord's, and upon them he has set the world."[4] The trap we fall into is thinking this is some event that happened in the past, rather than understanding that the pillars are, as you read this, being erected by God. If we think the world is a done deal, then it follows that the foundations must already be in place, but when we realize that the world is, even now, in the process of creation, then we recognize that it is possible that the foundations themselves are in the process of being established.

This came into clearer focus for me during a

> It would follow that when God had completed his foundation, he would place something upon it. Thus we read in the 21st chapter of Revelation, "He carried me away in the Spirit to a great, high mountain and showed me the holy city Jerusalem, coming down out of heaven from God."[5]

3 Proverbs 9:1-3
4 1 Samuel 2:8
5 Revelation 21:10

time when I had been considering the implications of the fact that Christ brought truth.[6] Where was truth before that? I had always thought of truth as an absolute of our temporal world, an inseparable part of creation, but that didn't fit the data. If Christ needed to bring truth, it wasn't here before.

Anyways, the thought that hit me was that this grace and truth that are spoken of are the pillars on which the church age is founded. The product, the result, of this age is righteousness, which is why Christ returns in righteousness,[7] at the completeness of this age. Malachi speaks of this as the time when the sun of righteousness will rise.[8]

Every millennia is established upon a pillar, for a total of seven pillars. Two pillars, or two millennia, make an age. In this we find the grouping of 2:2:2:1 that we left off last chapter during the discussion about the seven Spirits of God. This grouping orders as follows:

2	pillars	Adam to Abraham
2	pillars	Abraham to Christ
2	pillars	Christ to the Millennial Reign
1	pillar	Millennial Reign

I am going to name this the *pattern of foundation.*

Let us take a short stroll here, as this pattern hinges upon man's walk with God. The inference of Eden is that God walked with Adam.[9] After Adam disobeyed the commandment, this changed. We next read of Enoch[10] and Noah[11] walking with God. Then there is another change

6 John 1:17
7 Galatians 5:5, Revelation 19:11, Acts 17:31
8 Malachi 4:2
9 Genesis 3:8-10
10 Genesis 5:22
11 Genesis 6:9

in the time of Abraham, as we read in what is perhaps the most profound verse in the whole Bible.[12] Now Abraham is commanded to walk before God. Solomon speaks of those who walk before God in his prayer of dedication over the temple.[13] Then came Jesus Christ, and he tells us that he goes on ahead of us.[14] So the church age has been a time of God walking before man.

?	Eden	God walks with man
2 pillars	Adam to Abraham	Man walks with God
2 pillars	Abraham to Christ	Man walks before God
2 pillars	Christ to the Millennial Reign	God walks before man
1 pillar	Millennial Reign	?

With the turning of each age came a fundamental change in the way God related to men. In the Garden of Eden, Adam met God in a particular way. This changed when Adam ate from the tree of the knowledge of good and evil. Two thousand years later, God, through Abraham, began the establishment of his people. This was the beginning of a new type of relationship.

We are told in Revelation 21:3 that, on the new earth, God will dwell with men. We can therefore infer that the millennial reign is a time of man dwelling with God. If that is the case, the promise Christ gives in the first part of John 14, "In my Father's house are many dwelling places," is a millennial promise.[15]

12 Genesis 17:1
13 2 Chronicles 6:14
14 John 14:3
15 John 14:2

Then, journeying forward two thousand years, the Son of God himself came to change the way man related to God. Now, two thousand years after that event, we are passing through the gate of not just the fulfillment of a promise of the past, but also the greatest change yet in God's relationship with men. Because this change is fundamental, it supersedes doctrines and fulfills covenants, just as the examples of the past display.

The pillar of the millennial period is called Kingdom. It is only in a time established upon Kingdom that justice can be accomplished and judgment done. When Christ came to earth the first time, it was to accomplish righteousness, therefore John the Baptist preached repentance leading to salvation. This time it is, "Thy Kingdom Come,"[16] and the John the Baptist of this hour will preach maturity leading to authority. Kingdom is about justice accomplished through authority.

We are told that righteousness and justice are the foundation of the throne of God,[17] indicating that the church age and the millennium are the basis of God's reign. So it appears that this reign is not completely established when the millennium age is entered, but rather it comes to its fulfillment through the process of the millennium. There is a link between the last three days — the church age and the millennium — just as the *pattern of revelation* indicates.

Let us now touch on several other examples of the *pattern of revelation* in scripture.

16 Matthew 6:10
17 Psalms 97:2

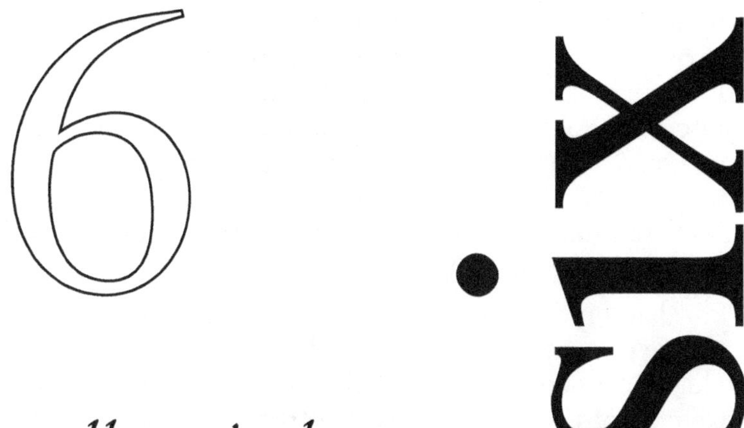

6 six

pattern instances

We have examined seven as the completion of the revelation of God, the unveiling of the mystery of the Most High. Paul speaks of Christ as the disclosing of the mystery of God,[1] so then shouldn't the *pattern of revelation* apply to him? Very astute observation, young grasshopper. And so it does. We read in Paul's first epistle to Timothy:[2]

Transgression & the Law

4 Great is the mystery of godliness
He was manifest in the flesh
Justified by the Spirit
Seen by angels

Church Age

2 Proclaimed among Gentiles
Believed in throughout the world

Millennium

1 Taken up in glory

Christ's association with the pattern is especially seen after his coming to earth. At that time, *Year 1*, there were

1 Romans 16:25-26
2 1 Timothy 3:16

three more days remaining to complete the revelation. Christ says of himself that he will spend three days and three nights in the heart of the earth.[3] As a fractal, that statement holds true both in the microscopic, the three days surrounding his death and resurrection, as well as the macroscopic, the three millennia yet to follow his birth. The last three days of the pattern are the theme we will move to in the next chapter.

In chapter three we spoke of the imagery of a folded piece of paper, which described how the *pattern of times* folded in upon itself. In Hebrews there is an excellent example of this, an example that proclaims both the old and new covenants.[4]

4
A mountain that can be touched
A blazing fire
A blackness
Darkness

2
A tempest
The sound of a trumpet

1
The voice of words

1
Mount Zion, the city of God, the Heavenly Jerusalem

2
Innumerable angels in festal assembly
The Church of the firstborn enrolled in heaven

4
God, the Judge of all
Spirits of righteous men made perfect
Jesus, mediator of a better covenant
The sprinkled blood, speaking a word better than Abel

3 Matthew 12:40
4 Hebrews 12:18–24

The pattern here runs 4:2:1:1:2:4, the first pattern runs forwards, the second runs backwards. This is somewhat like a Rorschach image. The first pattern speaks of the old covenant, the second of the new.

The pattern of 2:2:2:1, the *pattern of foundation,* is also seen here. For example, the first iteration divides out as follows:

2 A mountain that can be touched
A blazing fire

2 A blackness
Darkness

2 A tempest
The sound of a trumpet

1 The voice of words

You can see a relationship in each group. These relationships speak of the theme of each of the ages of the earth. And, in coming to an understanding of the themes of the past and how they applied, we are then ready to recognize, prepare for and respond to the themes of the future. This pattern can be collapsed into one greater pattern of 8:4:2. In this case the center would be applied to the beginning in this fashion:

> The phrase, "A mountain that can be touched," speaks of the temporal nature of the mountain, but not of the wisdom of such an action. Exodus 19:12 says that whoever touches the mountain will be put to death. So the dichotomy here is between a physical mountain which is out of reach, and a spiritual mountain which is within your grasp.

A mountain that can be touched	Mount Zion
A blazing fire	The voice of words

Now other themes begin to emerge. You can see reference to God calling Moses from the burning bush[5] in the joining of, *A blazing fire — The voice of words.* This was not just some arbitrary way to get Moses' attention, but displays a revelatory characteristic of the Most High. What is it telling us?

Let us take a look at another instance.[6] This is an especially good instance of the types. The 4:2:1, the *pattern of revelation,* and the 2:2:2:1, the *pattern of foundation,* are both easily discernible here.

4
Gilead is mine
Manasseh is mine
Ephraim is my helmet
Judah is my scepter

2
Moab is my washbasin
Upon Edom I cast my shoe

1
Over Philistia I shout in triumph

Remember that the information held in any instance of the pattern applies to every instance of the pattern. By this, one gains greater understanding both of the part and of the whole. For example, here both Moab and Edom encompass the church age. A study of Moab and Edom will aid in an understanding of the church age, and a study of the church age will help in an understanding of Moab and Edom.

Let us carry this a bit farther. When David was was moving the ark of the Lord to the tent that David had pitched for it, the scripture says that those who carried the ark went six paces, then David sacrificed to the Lord.[7] Whether these six paces were six steps, six kilometres or six leagues is immaterial to our discussion, for the six itself tells us that the story had moved to our time, six paces into the *pattern of revelation*. Where was the ark when they

5 Exodus 3:2 - 4
6 Psalms 108:8 - 9
7 2 Samuel 6:12 - 19

started their journey? We are told that it was in the house of Obed-edom (servant of Edom), whom the Lord blessed because of his care taking.

The history of the last thousand years is one of a renaissance of art and science, a renaissance that was meant for the people of God. Luther's re-establishment of faith set the stage. But then the ark, that "one new man,"[8] was touched. The Jewish people were rejected. And so that renaissance has remained with the servants of the world, the house of Obed-edom. In many ways our current position reminds me of the dwarfs in C.S. Lewis' *The Last Battle*. The world was being fundamentally altered, but they locked themselves inside a room, denying the changes going on around them, while exclaiming, "The Dwarfs are for the Dwarfs."[9]

Another instance. For this one we turn back to the book of Daniel.[10] Again, the time of Daniel, at the center of the pattern, reaffirms and elaborates upon that which was spoken of in the beginning.

Seventy sevens are decreed for
your people and your holy city
4 To finish the transgression
To put an end to sin
To atone for iniquity

2 To bring in everlasting righteousness
To seal both vision and prophet

1 To anoint a most holy one

Again, remember the fractal nature of the pattern. This speaks both of the greater *pattern of revelation*, the process of creation that we are currently walking through, but also speaks of a more specific instance of the pattern. You can take the elements of any iteration of the pattern, and bring

8 Ephesians 2:13-16
9 C.S. Lewis, *The Complete Chronicles of Narnia*, Collins, 1998, First American Edition, p. 511.
10 Daniel 9:24

them to bear on this one in order to gain a better understanding, and vice versa.

We also see that the final week — the final seven[11] — is cut in half; therefore the "abomination which desolates" that happens at the mid-point, is actually a reaffirmation and a fulfillment of the covenant which was struck at the beginning of the seven, as well as indicating that there is an important parallel between the years of tribulation and the *pattern of times.*

The language of the book of Daniel is difficult to parse, and I have not yet been shown one key which makes everything easily fall into place; however, greater understanding is now within reach, and through that understanding will come the uncovering of yet more mysteries.

Finally, let us deal with the restorative power of revelation. Peter speaks of Christ as remaining in heaven until the restoration of all things, which was declared by God through his holy prophets since the world began.[12] The culmination of revelation is restoration. The millennium brings restoration. The framework of creation is restoration. This begs the question, restoration of what? How could things begin with the idea of restoration? Doesn't something first have to be taken or be missing? This raises questions with answers of pre-creation implications, but that's not somewhere we will journey now.

The reign of Solomon speaks of the millennial reign. Solomon's name (Hebrew *shelomoh*) means *peaceable.*[13] Solomon is the *Prince of Peace.* And the Lord gives to Solomon the *pattern of all things*, the *pattern of revelation* as it applies to restoration.[14] God says that if his people will:

11 Daniel 9:27
12 Acts 3:21
13 Unger, Merrill F, "Solomon," *Unger's Bible Dictionary*, Moody Press, 1971.
14 2 Chronicles 7:14

4 Humble themselves
Pray
Seek my face
Turn from their wicked ways

2 I will hear from heaven
I will forgive their sin

1 I will heal their land

There are a lot of opinions out there on how to practice humbleness. It is interesting to note that this particular pattern shows turning from wickedness, the center of the pattern, as the fulfillment of humbleness. This means Moses, as the most humble man who ever lived,[15] must have lived a life in which he turned from evil. The writer of Hebrews affirms this when it is said that Moses refused to be called a son of Egypt, but [turned and] suffered with the people of God rather than enjoying the pleasures of sin.[16] Genesis speaks of a turning as one of the barriers God erects to prevent Adam from re-entering Eden.[17] There is a connection between these two turnings.

Moses life was divided into three parts, each lasting forty years. The first forty he spent in Egypt, the second forty were spent as a shepherd in Midian, the final forty were spent in the wilderness with the children of Israel. Moses never entered the promise. Notice the parallel between Moses and the 2:2:2:1 *pattern of foundation*. Moses lived through three ages, but never entered the inheritance. Joshua came alongside during the third age (Jesus is Greek for Joshua),[18] and it was Joshua who entered. Recognize then, that the church age is not as different from that which came before as we like to think. It is the time of the promise which brings the most significant change in the ages of the earth.

15 Numbers 12:3
16 Hebrews 11:24-25
17 Genesis 3:24
18 More accurately, the English is a transliteration of the Greek, which is a transliteration of the Hebrew.

Now, let us zoom in on a part of the *pattern of revelation,* in particular the last three days.

seven

the belly of the beast

How much can you accomplish in three days? How momentous a change can you effect? How lasting a legacy can you leave? Regardless of the strength of your right arm, I guarantee that your best efforts will pale in comparison to what the Son of Man brought about in that short a span. In three days, death gave way to victory.

The final three days of the pattern are the church age and the millennial reign. Christ mentioned these three days when he told his disciples that he would be killed and raised again on the third day.[1] He also declared that he could build up the temple of God in three days.[2] Having understood Christ's words, the chief priests and Pharisees wanted the tomb to be made secure until the third day.[3]

1 Matthew 20:17 - 19; Luke 18:31 - 33
2 John 2:19
3 Matthew 27:62 - 66

There is debate about the statement Christ makes, "For just as Jonah was three days and three nights in the belly of the beast, so for three days and three nights the Son of Man will be in the heart of the earth."[4]

Some say that this means he was in the grave for three full days, starting the count at the hour which he died. Others may point to Paul, who states, "...he was raised on the third day in accordance with the scriptures."[5] Paul says, "on the third day," not, "after the third day." Arguments fly back and forth like tennis balls. But which scriptures were Paul speaking about when he said that this occurred in accordance with the scriptures?

Probably the most direct is found in the book of Hosea, where the prophet calls:[6]

Come, let us return to the Lord;
for it is he who has torn, and he will heal us;
he has struck down, and he will bind us up.
After two days he will revive us;
on the third day he will raise us up,
that we may live before him.

Here we can see the relationship between the last three children of Leah that we spoke of in the second chapter. The three days are linked, but the third is different than the first two, just as Issachar, Zebulun and Dinah were siblings, but Dinah was the only girl among the boys. The first two days are spoken of as days of death. At the end of those two days life returns, and with the third day comes a raising up, a bringing to authority.

This is the pattern that Isaiah sees when prophesying to Hezekiah:[7]

This year eat what grows of itself,
In the second year what springs from that,

4 Matthew 12:39-40
5 1 Corinthians 15:4
6 Hoseah 6:1-2
7 Isaiah 37:30

In the third year sow, reap, plant vineyards and eat their fruit.

The first two years yield of themselves, but the third year brings the fulfillment of promise.

It is this transition that Peter warns us about.[8] He speaks of scoffers, which, as you may remember, are those within the camp of believers who deny the Spirit. These scoffers question the "promise of his coming." This is important. They don't question the coming of the Lord, they question the promise of his coming. And the promise of his coming is the Holy Spirit of God. As a believer you are sealed with the Holy Spirit of Promise.[9] When that seal is opened and that Spirit comes forth, there will be a great transformation. The land will no longer yield of itself, but rather the time of the fulfillment of promise has begun, the time of the possession of inheritance. Yet these scoffers will say that ever since our ancestors fell asleep, all things continue as they ever have been. They deny any change has come and refuse to be a participant in that change, just like the Dwarfs in Lewis' story.

This is the reason that believers have needed the Spirit of the Lord upon them as a separate act. The Spirit that lives within is sealed. He works transformatively within you, but his power cannot rest upon you from his presence. When that seal is broken, the power within you will then also become the power upon you. This is what it means when it says that Christ had the Spirit without limit.[10] There was no seal. There was nothing preventing the Spirit that was in him from also resting upon him. It has been impossible for men to minister in the manner of Christ because of this barrier. But when the barrier is gone, then

8 2 Peter 3:3-4
9 Ephesians 1:13
10 John 3:34

we shall see the fulfillment of the promise that we shall do even greater works than him because of his continual intercession for us.[11]

That seal was broken during his time in the wilderness. Christ went into that wilderness full of the Spirit, but he left filled with the power of the Spirit.[12] Power isn't strength, it is the ability to discipline, control and understand strength.

My sister-in-law is by no means a large girl in either height or frame. That is probably the reason people find it hard to believe that she used to participate in the sport of arm wrestling. When she was fourteen she went to the world championships, winning second with her left arm and first with her right. To top it off, she was competing in a weight class almost 50% heavier than her own when she wrestled with her left arm. It wasn't strength that made her successful, it was power — the ability to utilize the strength she had to greatest advantage.

When Christ was filled with the Spirit he was filled with strength. When he left the wilderness he knew how to use that strength. And that is what will bring us out of our wilderness — discipline, control and understanding of God's Spirit within us.

My background has taught me that the world is spiraling down into a morass of sin and evil, and, at the last it gets so bad that the saved are only hanging on by their fingernails and have to be raptured out of the whole filthy mess. This is something I no longer believe, for, where sin abounds, grace does much more abound.[13] And, not this only, but, where grace does much more abound, there also sin abounds. In other words, that which restrains,[14] restrains all. Evil is not restrained without there being a restraint upon righteousness. When that which restrains is removed, that which has been sealed up is released. Sin

11 John 14:12; Hebrews 7:25
12 Luke 4:1-14
13 Romans 5:20
14 2 Thessalonians 2:6-7

will then abound, but grace will much more abound. The sons of God shall enter their promise.

Now let us carry on, and dig into some scripture with this three day pattern laid out before us.

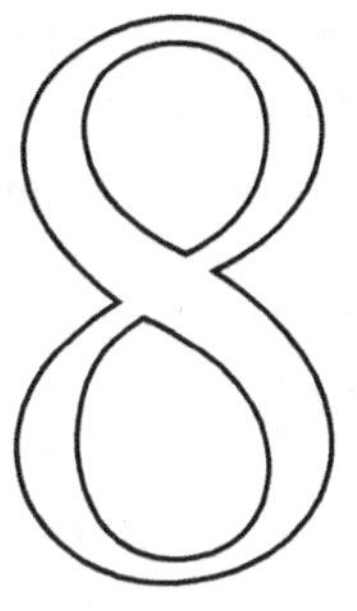

eight

the broad place

You shouldn't be surprised to learn that part of the language of God is mathematics. Peoples attitudes toward and understanding of math have certainly deemed it confusing, almost incomprehensible. Yet it is a language, and can be learned. Some concepts that appear to describe God, like infinite, are best spoken of in this language.

The introduction made mention of first principles and of how a body of knowledge is often based on building upon a framework of understanding. The opposite is seen when we bandy about descriptors of God, such as "God is unlimited," with no knowledge of the meaning or implications of such a statement, then happily declare the opposite five minutes later. Before we make such human declarations about who God is, it would be helpful to have some structure to work inside. Like it or not, mathematics is more than helpful, it is a necessary part of that structure.

If you have any post-secondary mathematics under your belt, there is a good chance you have debated the question of whether mathematics was created or discovered. Is mathematics intrinsic to the world in which we live, or a tool we have created that helps us to examine this world? The scriptures describe God as being One.[1] Like the other characteristics of God, it is something we are urged to become.[2] Yet, what does it mean? Our problems with the Trinity of God stem not from some true philosophical or empirical problem of three being one, but rather speak of our own profound ignorance of the spiritual landscape upon which God lives. When we say "God is Love," we view it as an internal characteristic, a part of his nature. When we say, "God is One," we view it as an external characteristic, part of his physical makeup. The problem is that the idea of an external characteristic has the implication of *more than one*. What I mean is that any physical descriptor assumes someone else is there to see, someone outside to look upon this characteristic — a *two*, as it were. Such a view is probably erroneous, and to say that God is One is to speak of his intrinsic nature, not just the sum of God and his being either singular or plural.

Andrew Hodges writes that, "English uses almost the same symbol for *I*, the first person, as for *One*; and its pronoun *one* stands for the impersonal *I*. We look after *number one*; the sole soul. But the individual's One-ness is not a static quality, but a process, a dialogue, perhaps an intense struggle."[3] A better stab at what it means to be *one* than most.

There is no real math in what we are doing here, outside of some feebly basic addition and subtraction and a ratio or two. Numbers in this text are really placeholders, describing a spiritual landscape for which we do not have words. Some see such an exercise as numerology. But consider the weight which lies upon a word like *grace*. We

1 James 2:19
2 John 17:22-23
3 Andrew Hodges, *One To Nine: The Inner Life of Numbers*, Doubleday, 1st Canadian Publishing, 2007, p. 34.

do not redefine grace upon its own rights every time we encounter that word in the text of the scriptures. Rather, each instance we examine adds to our understanding of grace as a whole, and can be applied to any instance where the bible speaks of grace. Why should we find it difficult to imagine that such a relationship could be had among the numerals, and that any mention of three adds to our greater understanding of what the text is saying?

With that in mind we turn to Genesis and the life of Issac. At the time we look in on him, his father Abraham had died, and his two sons, Jacob and Esau, had been born. There was a famine, and Isaac had settled in the land of the Philistines. God had blessed Isaac after the death of his father Abraham,[4] and Isaac's time in the land of the Philistines was very fruitful.

Isaac is known as the son of promise,[5] and a parallel can be drawn between Isaac and Jesus Christ. At this point in Isaac's story, we will begin paralleling the text with scripture about Christ, for there are three wells mentioned in Isaac's story, and that number should now begin to draw our attention.

1a. Issac:

The wells of Abraham, dug by his servants, had been stopped up by the Philistines. This deprived both themselves and others of the ability to draw water to drink.[6]

1b. Jesus:

The powers of the world had filled the wells of salvation, dug by the servants of the old covenant, depriving both themselves and others of drawing and drinking of that salvation.[7]

4 Genesis 25:11
5 Romans 9:8-9
6 Genesis 26:15
7 Matthew 23:13; Isaiah 12:3

2a. Issac:

The son of promise was mightier than the Philistines and was rejected by the Philistines.[8]

2b. Jesus:

The Son of Promise was mightier than the world and was rejected by the world.[9]

3a. Issac:

The king of the Philistines came against the son of promise and he departed into the valley.[10]

3b. Jesus:

The prince of the world came against the Son of Promise and he departed into the valley.[11]

4a. Issac:

The son of promise remade the stopped up wells and called them by the names spoken by his father.[12]

4b. Jesus:

The Son of Promise remade the way, fulfilling that calling spoken of by his Father and giving all who enter a name from his Father.[13]

In this valley, the servants of Isaac dug two wells. Both were taken by the herders of the Philistines. Issac's servants then dug yet another, and on this third well the Philistines had no claim.

For two thousand years the blessing and work of the servants of the Christ has been contended (*Esek*), and been at enmity (*Sitnah*), with the world. The last two thousand years are those two wells. But the threshold has been crossed and the time has come to dig the third well.

8 Genesis 26:16
9 John 16:33, Isaiah 53:3
10 Genesis 26:16 - 17
11 John 14:30, Psalm 23:4
12 Genesis 26:18
13 Hebrews 10:20 [*egkainizo* - to do anew], Matthew 5:17, Revelation 2:17

This one will be ours, our "Broad Place" (*Rehoboth*). It is time to enter the inheritance.

Again, I say that the *pattern of revelation* informs us that this will be the greatest change yet seen in God's relationship with men. Be prepared to be unprepared. Most of us will dislike this change, for it is going to begin shaking loose the misconceptions we have about God, and many of those misconceptions are our *unshakable doctrines*. Watchman Nee says that all truth is humbling.[14] That is why we have such a difficult time accepting truth, for it attacks our pride.

The Broad Place insight can be carried throughout scripture in order to help glean information about the time we are entering into. Previously, I mentioned Solomon's insight into the state of the church at this hour. One reason we can theorize that he was speaking of this time is that he writes that wisdom calls from the Broad Place,[15] at the entrance of the gates. This is how we know the word about the simple, scoffer and fool is for today, the time in which we are entering that Broad Place.

Isaiah speaks of the emergence of the one who will declare the way.[16] At that time every valley will be lifted up and every mountain made low. This is a reference to that Broad Place. The lowering of mountains and the raising of valleys can be traced through scripture to give you a better understanding of the time we have entered.

David saw this place into which we have passed, and you can see his insight in passages such as, "He brought me out into a broad place; he delivered me, because he delighted in me,"[17] and in Psalm 26, where he asks for justice (a future event, the millennium), declares righteousness (a event which is completed, the church age), then finishes by stating, "My foot stands on level ground; in the congregation I will bless the Lord."[18]

14 Watchman Nee, *A Table in the Wilderness*, Tyndale House Publishers, 1965, 1981, May 16th Devotional.
15 Proverbs 1:20-21 *Rehobe*, here translated as street[s]
16 Isaiah 40:3-5
17 Psalm 18:19
18 Psalm 26:12

I love this topic and find it difficult to move beyond, so let's take time for one more reference. In his discourse with Job, Elihu mentions this time when he says, "He also allured you out of distress into a broad place where there is no constraint, and what was set on your table was full of fatness."[19] A promise that is mind-boggling in its implications. A place of ever expanding boundaries, full of the Spirit of God.

19 Job 36:16

nine

tools of the trade

So, you've been provoked into doing some scriptural spelunking. Excellent. But every task is made easier with better tools.

Most carpenters carry a hand plane in their toolboxes, but they generally see little use. The reason is that few people, in this age of power tools, have learned how to sharpen a blade. Yet a well sharpened hand plane has no power tool replacement. I trust that you will find here a few well sharpened blades.

Dust

The word *dust* is very evocative. Just hearing someone say dust makes you want to blow your nose. I have lived in desert-like climates for most of my life and have, in the last few years, lived through an extended drought. In drought, one gains a new understanding of the pervasiveness of dust. In wetter climes, conditions may distract dust from being the center of attention, but it is always there under your nose.

Dust is also an important topic in the scriptures and has a definite meaning. Let us take a look at a few places where dust is mentioned.

Job speaks of two men, one who dies in the fullness of his strength and a second who dies in the bitterness of his soul. Yet both of these, Job says, lie down in the dust.[1] Isaiah speaks of the nations of the earth being as dust on a scale in the accounting of God.[2] Solomon tells us that the end of a thing is seen in the dust returning to the earth from where it came.[3]

One doesn't need to chase dust through the scriptures for very long before you notice the theme of temporality emerge. To speak of dust is to speak of that which will pass away, that which is not eternal, and recognizing the implications of dust aids in our understanding of many passages of scripture.

Before looking at a particular example, I will branch into covenant. Most of you reading this will already have been introduced to the concept of making covenant through a meal. There are many examples in the Bible. Esau passes his blessing to Jacob through a covenant meal.[4] God covenanted with the Israelites through the Passover meal.[5] The Scribes and Pharisees were upset with Christ for eating with sinners and tax collectors, because they understood that meant he was covenanting with them.[6] Christ introduces his new covenant during a Passover meal.[7]

Let us gather this understanding of dust and the covenant meal and take a trip back to the Garden of Eden. After the transgression of Adam, God makes a few pronouncements, and one of them was upon the serpent, the insti-

1 Job 21:23-26
2 Isaiah 40:15
3 Ecclesiastes 12:7
4 Genesis 25:29-34
5 Exodus 12
6 Luke 15:1-2
7 Matthew 26:26-29

gator of the beginning of the process. God declares that the serpent shall eat dust all the days of his life.[8] The natural result of the curse is that the serpent will spend his days in the dirt, but the spiritual result of the curse is that he will forever covenant with temporal things, things that pass away. None of his works will have any eternal existence.

Peter tells us that water is the primordial element of creation, and it is out of water that dust came.[9] And from this water and this dust, the soul and the flesh, came the clay of God with which he fashioned all things. Now, take what you know about dust, then sit back and consider scriptures such as Genesis 2:7. If and when the lights come on, you will recognize the implications. Much of what we thought we knew suddenly doesn't fit together anymore.

Mary, Mary

Mary is the Greek form of Miriam. It is possible to chase Marys through the Bible from Exodus onward. The two we are specifically interested in are Mary the mother of Jesus and Mary Magdalene.

Mary means *rebellion,* and Moses speaks of the Israelites as those who have been rebellious ever since God has known them.[10] The correlation I am making here is one between the Israelites and Mary, the mother of Jesus Christ.

We are told that a man shall leave his mother and father and be joined to his bride.[11] This applied to the first Adam, and so it also applies to the second Adam.[12] We know that Christ left his father, God, but in order to fulfill prophecy it is necessary that he also leave his mother. Does this mean the Jewish people? John tells us that Christ came

8 Genesis 3:14
9 2 Peter 3:5
10 Deuteronomy 9:24
11 Genesis 2:24
12 1 Corinthians 15:35 - 49

to his own people and they did not receive him, but to those who do receive him he gives the power to become a son of God.[13] The apostle Paul speaks of the blinding of the Jews that veils the identity of their Messiah from their eyes.[14] Christ left the Jewish people with the ultimate aim of being joined to his bride.

What does this tell us? When Paul reiterates the commandment to honour your father and mother,[15] spiritually he is speaking of God and the Jewish people. The history of the relationship between the church and the Jewish people is not one the church can look to with pride. Remember, though, that this history shows off the times of contention and enmity through which the church has passed. But now, as the sons of God enter the Broad Place, the coming of the Lord is displayed by the breaking down of the barrier between Greek and Jew, by the infusion of peace, by the creation of that one new man.[16]

Second, there is Mary Magdalene, the *rebellious one of the tower.* This is a reference to those who come out of the body of Christ. We see, then, that the first Mary is the Jewish people, and the second Mary is the bride. This is a spiritual connection that has certainly been recognized by those outside the church, one example being Dan Brown's novel, *The Da Vinci Code.*

How does all this help us? Well, we know that Jesus left his mother in the care of his disciple, John,[17] therefore, if you know who John is, you have a good foundation to understand the history of the last two thousand years of the Jewish people. And consider the seven devils cast out of Mary Magdalene.[18] What does this tell us about the *pattern of revelation,* and how that pattern relates to the bride?

---

13 John 1:11 - 12
14 Romans 9 - 11
15 Ephesians 6:2
16 Ephesians 2:13 - 16
17 John 19:26 - 27
18 Mark 16:9

Mountain

Before we begin the topic of mountain, I would like to mention a Biblical construct I call *paralleling.* What this consists of is an idea, presented in scripture, alongside a way to accomplish or another way to view the idea. As an example let us look at Psalm 96:7-10:

Give to the Lord, O families of the people;
Give unto the Lord glory and strength,
Give unto the Lord the glory due his name.

Bring an offering and come into his courts,
Worship the Lord in the beauty of holiness,
Fear him all the earth.

Say among the nations, "The Lord reigns."

The parallels here are:

Give to the Lord, O families of the people;
Bring an offering and come into his courts

Give unto the Lord glory and strength,
Worship the Lord in the beauty of holiness

Give unto the Lord the glory due his name
Fear him all the earth

And the result of this is: *The Lord reigns.*

There are three directives in the first sentence. In the second sentence they are met with, in this case, three ways to accomplish those directives. Finally, a conclusion is offered. Again, these parallels give direction or add to the original idea presented. With that in mind, let us look at Micah 4:2-3:

a) Come, and let us go up to the mountain of the Lord
b) And to the house of the God of Jacob
c) That he may teach us his ways
d) That we may walk in his paths
e) For the law will go forth from Zion
f) And the word of the Lord from Jerusalem
g) And he will judge between many peoples

Our parallels here are:

a) Come and let us go up to the mountain of the Lord
c) That he may teach us his ways
e) For the law (or, instruction) will go forth from Zion

b) Let us go up to the house of the God of Jacob
d) That we may walk in his path
f) The word of the Lord will go forth from Jerusalem

The first and second lines are directives. The third and fourth lines, in this case, describe the reasons for the directives. The fifth and sixth lines are results and the seventh offers a conclusion. This is the *pattern of the mountain*. The first speaks of teaching, of instruction, and the second speaks of inheritance, of a passing on to others.

In support of the first we find that the scriptures speak of Christ teaching on the mountain[19] his great *Sermon on the Mount*. We read that he went up the mountain, sat down, his disciples came to him, and then he began to teach them. God summoned Moses to the top of Mount Sinai to instruct him on the law.[20] The temple, the house of instruction, was built by Solomon upon Mount Moriah.[21]

In support of the second we find the Lord giving Elijah direction on inheritance, about the passing on of leadership and Elijah's own prophetic mantle, upon Mount Horeb.[22] King Saul was slain upon Mount Gilboa, and

19 Matthew 5:1 - 2
20 Exodus 19
21 2 Chronicles 3:1
22 1 Kings 19:11 - 18

kingship passed on to David.[23] Jesus Christ charges his disciples with the mandate of the church age upon Mount Olivet.[24]

Leveling the mountains, as was discussed in the chapter on the Broad Place, speaks of preparing the way of the Lord.[25] It is a time of great changes in spiritual realms, just as the leveling of mountains show great changes in material realms. We are told that if you say to this mountain, "Be lifted up and thrown into the sea," it will be done.[26] Spiritually, this mountain is the instruction and inheritance we obtained from the first Adam, and these things are done away with when you confess Christ[27] [see *Sea*]. Upon our confession we become children of God, and, as children, we are then heirs to the things of God.[28] The Holy Spirit of God becomes our instructor, teaching us the eternal value of our inheritance.[29] We have not come to a mountain that can be touched, a teaching and an inheritance that is temporal in nature. Rather, we have come to Mount Zion, the city of the Living God, the heavenly Jerusalem.[30]

A verse in the book of Revelation calls for a mind that has wisdom, then speaks of the seven mountains on which the woman, the great harlot, is seated.[31] Many say that this is obviously Rome, which is built upon seven hills. If that truly is the greater significance, then why does the scripture call for a mind that has wisdom? Take what you now know about seven and about mountains, then see what you can derive from this passage.

---

23 1 Chronicles 10:8
24 Acts 1:6-12
25 Isaiah 40:3-5
26 Matthew 21:21
27 2 Corinthians 5:17
28 Romans 8:16-17
29 John 14:26
30 Hebrews 12:18,22; Exodus 19:10-15
31 Revelation 17:9

Numbering

My father is a carpenter, and, to a degree, I followed in his footsteps. One of the first concepts you are introduced to in construction is the importance of accurate measurements. The popular mantra is, "measure twice, cut once." For a lot of us that should be, "measure thrice."

The topic of accurate measurement is very interesting. I think the most measurement obsessed occupation I know of is that of the machinist. In construction, framing is accurate to about a quarter inch (0.25). For those of you who have had a bad experience with a contractor, I should say that it is supposed to be that accurate. In cabinetry you may try to work to 1/64th of an inch (~0.015). A machinist, though, will regularly spit out something about, "taking it down another thou" (0.001), with a 1/10000th (0.0001) being the grail.

I doubt God has near as much problem with accurate measurement as us; however, the act of measuring and counting have a particular spiritual meaning.

God says to Jeremiah that as the host of heaven cannot be counted, and as the sand of the sea cannot be measured, so he will multiply the descendants of David and the Levites.[32] God took Abraham outside and told him that if he could count all the stars, he would be able to count his descendants.[33] Eliphaz tells Job that God does great things without number.[34]

Even after these few examples we can see a pattern. If something is uncounted it does not come to an end. Therefore, a thing that is counted should be the opposite. Can we find any examples?

Job declares that God knows the number of the months of a man, that he has made a limit that cannot be passed.[35] When the hand writes on the wall during Belshazzar's feast, Daniel's interpretation of the writing begins with,

32 Jeremiah 33.22
33 Genesis 15:5
34 Job 5:9
35 Job 14:5

"God has numbered your kingdom and put an end to it."[36]

You can go and search out more examples for yourself, but I will state now that to measure is to place within limits, and to be unmeasured or immeasurable is to place outside limits. To number is to come to an end, to be without number is to be eternal. This helps us to understand why God was upset with David when he measured or numbered Israel and Judah.[37] He was taking God's eternal people[38] and bringing them to an end.

We read in Isaiah that God has put dust in a measure[39] — a temporary thing with a finite existence. This speaks of creation, and, even more specifically, of fleshly man.

Undoubtedly the most famous number in the Bible is the number of the beast.[40] John speculated that if all the acts of Jesus were written down the world could not contain the books.[41] Those writing about the number of the beast seemingly desire to make up for this egregious lack by filling the world with their books. It isn't my desire to add another tome; however, I can't resist adding a couple points of my own. What is immediately apparent is that because he has a number, he comes to an end. At this point one could speculate that the number itself, 666, tells you his measure, but I'll leave this for you to delve into if you are interested.

Sea

The sea is a fantastic place, an alien world in our own backyard. I have heard that we know more about how our solar system ticks than we know about the sea. The lack of breathable oxygen coupled with the immense pressures contribute to make an environment that is difficult for a

36 Daniel 5:26
37 2 Samuel 24:1
38 2 Samuel 7:24
39 Isaiah 40:12
40 Revelation 13:18
41 John 21:25

man to journey through. Yet the scenery certainly makes the effort worthwhile.

The smallest and the largest life forms on earth call the sea their home. It is the abode of some the the simplest and some of the most complex creatures on the planet. Arguably, the second most intelligent animal on the earth is a sea animal, to say nothing of the brain power displayed by the lowly invertebrate octopus.

I had read a piece written by Rick Joyner, and while it was running through my head, I suddenly realized that to speak of the sea was to speak of death. Actually, not specifically the sea, but the fact that the sea is salty. It is the salt that causes the sea to refer to death. Salt, combined with water — the form God takes in the natural — creates an environment in which the dead can live without dying, just as a *dead* man, a man without Christ, can live out a life on earth. We all live in a sea, in the "waters below."[42]

The significance of leaving Egypt is that the children of Israel were moving from death to life, and this is demonstrated by their passing through the sea, whereas the Egyptians are engulfed. We are told that at the time of the remaking of creation there will be no more sea,[43] and that death will be no more.[44] Jonah's *death* was displayed by his being cast into the heart of the seas.[45] Sin itself is put to death, for God casts it into the sea as well.[46]

The place of death in the millennium is mentioned in Ezekiel when he speaks of the swamps and marshes being left for salt.[47] Isaiah says that they will not hurt or destroy on the holy mountain, for the earth will be filled with the knowledge of the Lord, as the waters cover the sea.[48] Knowledge covers over death, which is why we are told that Christ justified many through his knowledge.[49] Christ

42 Genesis 1:7
43 Revelation 21:1
44 Revelation 21:4
45 Jonah 2:3
46 Micah 7:19
47 Ezekiel 47:11
48 Isaiah 11:9
49 Isaiah 53:11

tells the disciples that they will be fishers of men,[50] in other words, they are pulling those who live in death out to life.

We are called the salt and the light.[51] John tells us that in Jesus Christ was life, and that life was the light of men.[52] So we see that to be called salt and light is to be called death and life. Through death Christ laid hold of death[53] and now holds the keys of hell and death.[54] Our tongues have the power of life and of death.[55] As believers, we are the aroma of Christ unto God, a fragrance of death unto death for those who are perishing, and life unto life for those who are being saved.[56]

This leads to a few interesting verses to follow up on. We are told to worship him that made the sea.[57] The first beast of the Revelation rises up out of the sea.[58] But perhaps the most interesting is that God created the sea, then put the sea within boundaries.[59] That means when sin came through Adam's transgression, and death entered,[60] it wasn't that death came into being, but rather that death left its established boundaries. What were those boundaries, and how were they breached?

Valley

The valley was mentioned in Chapter 8. When the king of the Philistines came against Isaac, Isaac departed into the valley.[61] The valley refers to the church age.

50 Matthew 4:19
51 Matthew 5:13-14
52 John 1:4
53 Hebrews 2:14
54 Revelation 1:18
55 Proverbs 18:21
56 2 Corinthians 2:15-16
57 Revelation 14:7
58 Revelation 13:1
59 Job 38:8-11; Proverbs 8:29
60 Romans 5:12-14
61 Genesis 26:16-17

I call the 23rd Psalm *Gethsemane's Prayer,* because it seems to me that this is the prayer that Christ prayed in the Garden of Gethsemane ["You have set a table before me in the presence of my enemies," corresponds to, "She has also set her table," which is the introduction to the church age in that specific iteration of the pattern. See *Chapter* 5]. One line in that prayer states, "Yea, though I walk through the valley of the shadow of death."[62] Here we see Christ declaring that a new age has begun. This is reflective of the children of Israel passing through death to life, where the waters formed a wall for them on their right and on their left,[63] or, made a valley through the sea, just as the church age is a valley through death that leads to eternal life.

Moses was laid to rest in a valley in the land of Moab.[64] Moab, as seen previously, is reflective of one of the pillars of the church age, and the valley speaks of the church age. He was buried against Beth-Peor, or, the House of the Cleft, the place where one leaves the valley. Moses' journey lead him through the valley, but not out of it, and he died at the place where those called to the inheritance left the valley.

Ezekiel was brought into the middle of the valley.[65] The valley was full of dry bones. The church age runs two thousand years, so the mid-point would be about AD 1000. Of this period, Henry Halley writes, "The 200 years between Nicolas I and Gregory VII [867-1073] is called by historians the MIDNIGHT OF THE DARK AGES. Bribery, Corruption, Immorality and Bloodshed, make it just about the Blackest Chapter in the Whole History of the Church."[66] God's question to Ezekiel was, "Can these bones live?"[67] The following thousand years have been a history of the refashioning of those bones. Those bones

62 Psalm 23:4
63 Exodus 14:22
64 Deuteronomy 34:6
65 Ezekiel 37:1
66 Henry H. Halley, *Halley's Bible Handbook*, Zondervan Publishing House, 24th Edition © 1965, p. 774.
67 Ezekiel 37:3

have come together, the sinews have been placed upon them, the flesh and skin covered them. But there is no breath in them.[68]

This breath in the valley is that period referred to previously as *the promise of his coming.*

68 Ezekiel 37:7-8

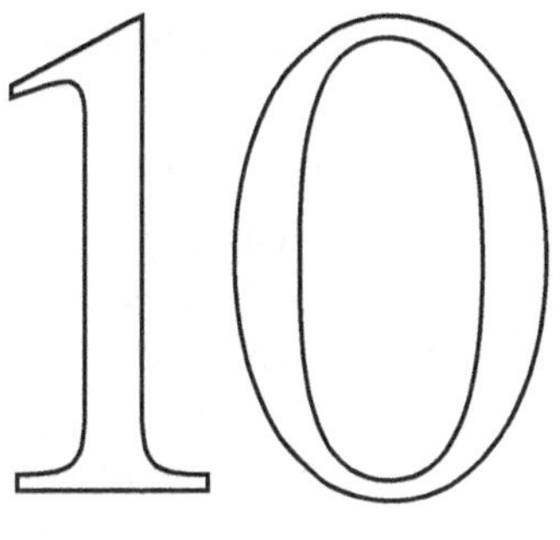

the body of christ

What does it mean to be *literal*? If you flip open your dictionary you will find some variation of, "using the common meaning of words to understand the intent." It is interesting that two people, purposing to take the Bible literally, will have such divided doctrines. The apostle Paul tells us that we now see through a glass, in a riddle,[1] so these types of disagreements shouldn't surprise us.

One point most literalists have missed is just how literally the statement that, "we are the body of Christ," is meant. Sitting in the big chair by the fireplace and contemplating this one day, it struck me that the body of Christ makes a three day journey, therefore the events of the crucifixion and resurrection should have parallels in church history.

I reached over and grabbed Halley's Bible Handbook. This is my father's copy, circa 1965. Newer editions have had much of his material at the end of the book removed, as well as revising his very interesting look at the Book of Revelation. This edition has a chapter on church history,

1 1 Corinthians 13:12

and I have pulled all the relevant events and dates from there.[2]

This first timeline plots a comparison between the two days of death surrounding the crucifixion and the two thousand years of church history. It is interesting how they seemingly mesh so well. Some of the events are, at least on the surface, a direct parallel. For example, on the cross a charge was posted against Christ, "This is the King of the Jews." The time of the cross correlates to the time when the head of the church became an earthly king.

To make sense of some of the other linked events, like the sealing of the tomb with the Reformation, we would need some additional information before we could claim any significant correlation.

Certainly, there is some speculation. For example, we are not given the time of Christ's betrayal. We could chart out the events and make an educated guess, calculating how long a time the meal, the hymn and the walk to the Mount of Olives took. I have placed the betrayal between 1:00-2:00 am, and there it conveniently links up with the paganization of the church.

But what if we can start overlaying timelines to give our speculations a bit more substance? Let us give it a try, using the life of Joseph.

2 Henry H. Halley, *Halley's Bible Handbook*, Zondervan Publishing House, 24th Edition © 1965, p. 757-804.

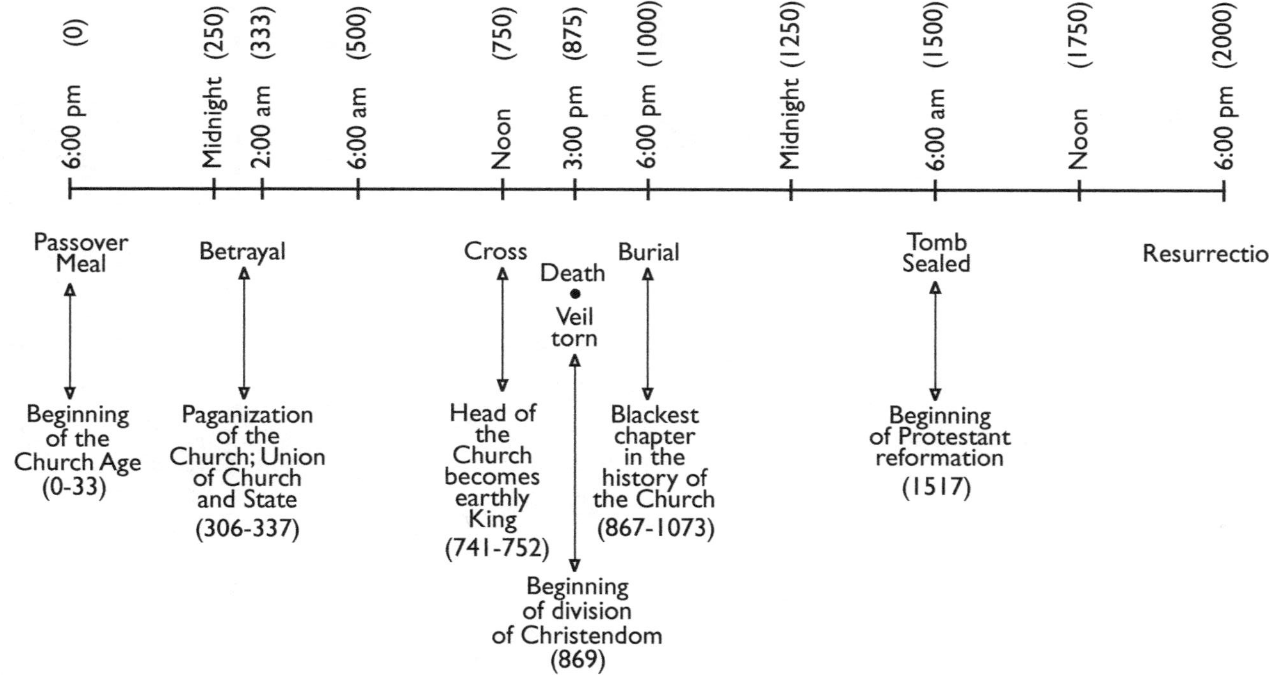
6:00 pm (0)
Midnight (250)
2:00 am (333)
6:00 am (500)
Noon (750)
3:00 pm (875)
6:00 pm (1000)
Midnight (1250)
6:00 am (1500)
Noon (1750)
6:00 pm (2000)
Passover Meal
Beginning of the Church Age (0-33)
Betrayal
Paganization of the Church; Union of Church and State (306-337)
Cross
Head of the Church becomes earthly King (741-752)
Death • Veil torn
Beginning of division of Christendom (869)
Burial
Blackest chapter in the history of the Church (867-1073)
Tomb Sealed
Beginning of Protestant reformation (1517)
Resurrection

Joseph lived to the ripe old age of 110.[3] Let us take his life and stretch it out over the length of our timeline. Joseph was betrayed by his brethren at 17 years of age.[4] When we place this on his timeline, it lines up with the betrayal of Christ and the paganization of the church.

This isn't a proof; however, the alignment is notable. Let us take a look at one more, involving the ark of the covenant.

3 Genesis 50:26
4 Genesis 37

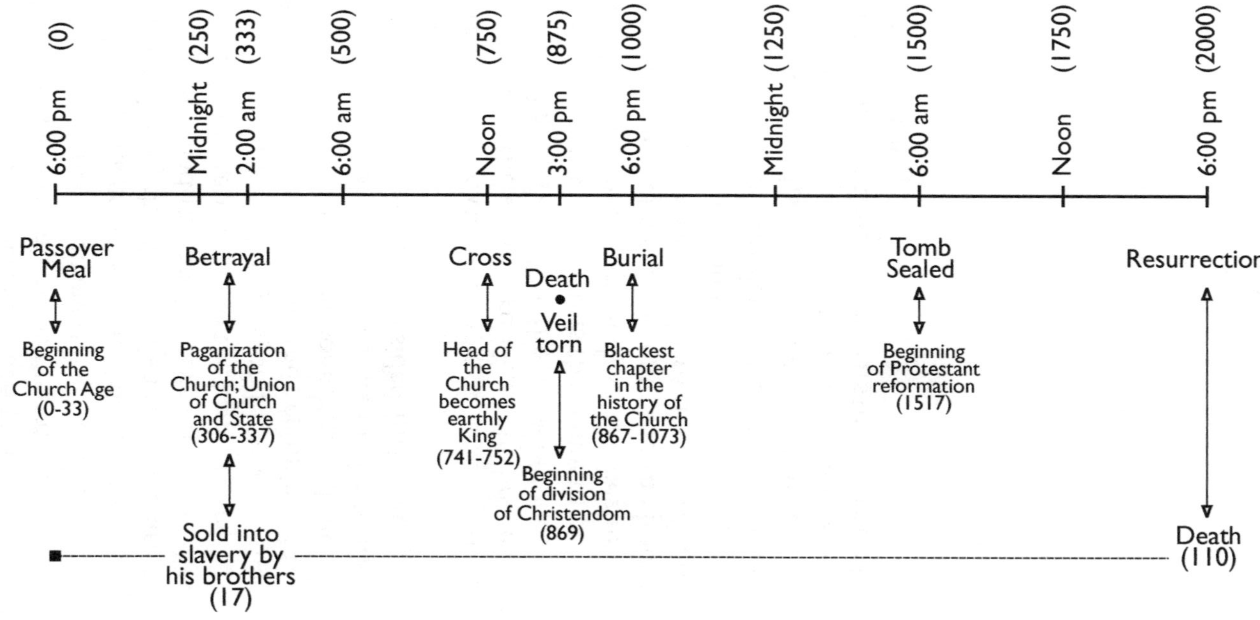
6:00 pm (0)
Midnight (250)
2:00 am (333)
6:00 am (500)
Noon (750)
3:00 pm (875)
6:00 pm (1000)
Midnight (1250)
6:00 am (1500)
Noon (1750)
6:00 pm (2000)
Passover Meal
Beginning of the Church Age (0-33)
Betrayal
Paganization of the Church; Union of Church and State (306-337)
Sold into slavery by his brothers (17)
Cross
Head of the Church becomes earthly King (741-752)
Death
Veil torn
Beginning of division of Christendom (869)
Burial
Blackest chapter in the history of the Church (867-1073)
Tomb Sealed
Beginning of Protestant reformation (1517)
Resurrection
Death (110)

For this iteration, a period of one year is stretched over the timeline. On this twelve month segment we will place two incidents involving the ark of the covenant.

The first happens when the ark is captured by the Philistines during the days of Samuel.[5] We are told that the Philistines had the ark for seven months.[6] Let us say that the ark was betrayed into the hands of the Philistines through the wicked lifestyles of Eli's sons, the priests Hophni and Phinehas. Placing the beginning of this seven month period at the betrayal point, the full seven months carry us to the point of the sealing of the tomb and the Reformation. The ark then resided in Kiriath-jearim for twenty years.[7]

By that time, David was king of Israel, and he determined to move the ark to Jerusalem. His first attempt was a bust and the ark was left in the home of Obed-Edom for three months.[8] If we place this three month period at the end of the seven month period, so the beginning corresponds with the sealing of the tomb and the Reformation, the three months carry us right to the end of the year, to the time of the resurrection.

In Chapter Six a correlation was drawn between the Renaissance, at its high point by the time of the Reformation, and the ark of the covenant residing with Obed-Edom. This timeline appears to lend a bit of support to that argument.

5 1 Samuel 4
6 1 Samuel 6:1
7 1 Samuel 7:2
8 2 Samuel 6:11

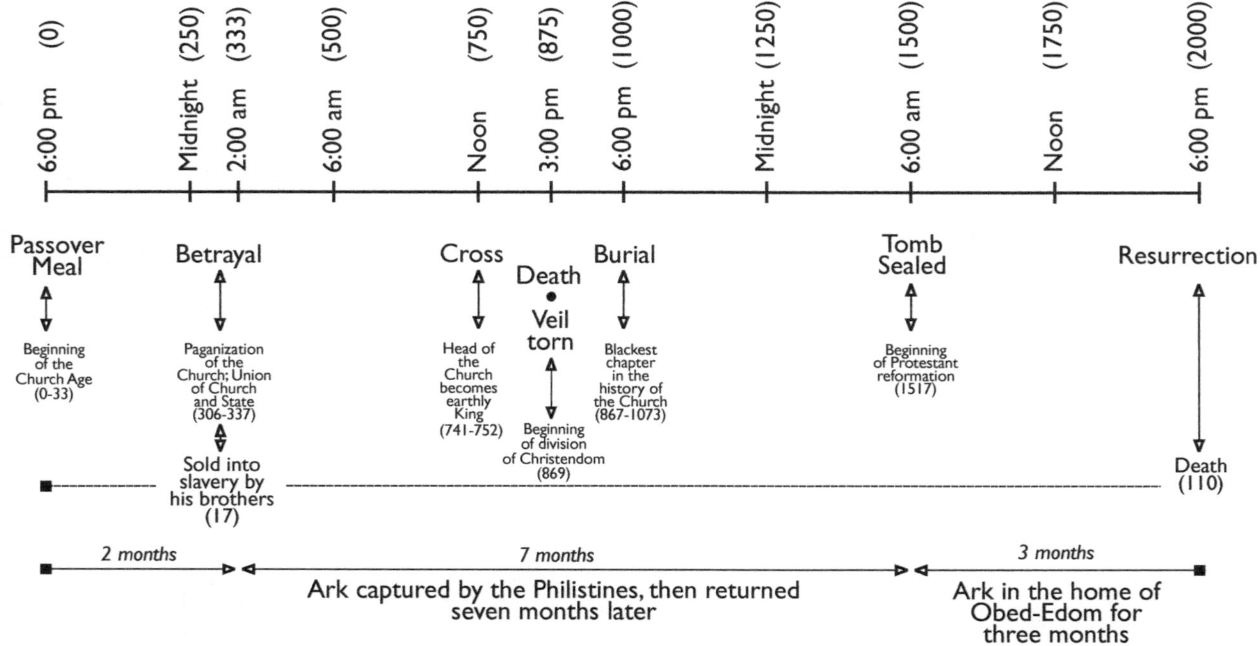

6:00 pm (0)
Midnight (250)
2:00 am (333)
6:00 am (500)
Noon (750)
3:00 pm (875)
6:00 pm (1000)
Midnight (1250)
6:00 am (1500)
Noon (1750)
6:00 pm (2000)
Passover Meal
Beginning of the Church Age (0-33)
Betrayal
Paganization of the Church; Union of Church and State (306-337)
Cross
Head of the Church becomes earthly King (741-752)
Death • Veil torn
Beginning of division of Christendom (869)
Burial
Blackest chapter in the history of the Church (867-1073)
Tomb Sealed
Beginning of Protestant reformation (1517)
Resurrection
Sold into slavery by his brothers (17)
Death (110)
2 months
7 months
3 months
Ark captured by the Philistines, then returned seven months later
Ark in the home of Obed-Edom for three months

GH Hardy is quoted as saying to Bertrand Russell, "If I could prove by logic that you would die in five minutes, I should be sorry you were going to die, but my sorrow would be very much mitigated by pleasure in the proof."[9] What you have here is neither proof nor an attempt at a proof, but I see the edge of something important, and it certainly deserves to be followed up. I have had little insight in this regard, but perhaps someone reading this will begin to see the pattern.

9 Robert Kanigel, *The Man Who Knew Infinity*, Washington Square Press, 1991, p. 224.

11

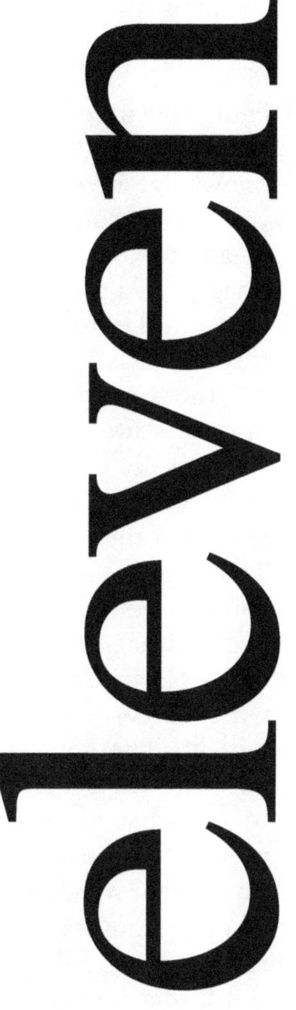

the sum

A circle is the compression of the infinite into the finite. We are told that the word is without constraint[1] and that it endures forever.[2] It is the infinite, given to us in a compressed, finite form. It is the glory of God to conceal a matter, and the glory of Kings to search it out.[3] To come to a better understanding of God it is necessary for us to come to an understanding of how to open the finite in order that the infinite comes forth.

You may now be wondering about the relevance of what you have been reading. How is this going to impact you? How is it going to change and grow your relationship with God? Even if they are true, why are the patterns important, and where is an understanding of pattern going to take you?

1 2 Timothy 2:9
2 1 Peter 1:25
3 Proverbs 25:2

Paul is struck blind on the road to Damascus.[4] This isn't a story about him losing his sight, it is a story about him being made aware of his real condition. The God Paul proclaimed wasn't who Paul thought he was. In the beginning knowledge brings a wrestling with God, because knowledge reveals a God quite unfamiliar with the one you have become comfortable with. But then, man wasn't meant to dwell in a garden. "Let us make man in our image,"[5] is a process, not an event. That is why, after they ate from the tree and obtained knowledge, God says, "See, the man has become like one of us."[6] And that process continues to carry us inexorably forward, to the measure of the stature of the fullness of Christ.[7]

Hopefully you have begun to realize that the way God works isn't a collection of unrelated moments, but that there is a theme, a line that runs through all of creation.[8] That line is God's pattern. When you recognize pattern you have a foundation to understand what has come before and to imagine what is to come. You will have become aware of the first principles, the underlying structure upon which theories can be tested and into which knowledge will fit. The conformation of events around you to the pattern will reveal the hand of God. You will be able to see what he is doing. If you want to understand the measure of the days in which we are living and see the age into which we are moving, you must know the pattern.

When you read that Christ did only what he saw the Father doing, what image comes to your mind? Do you think that he continuously saw visions of the Father and duplicated this vision, or does this speak of something more? I believe he had learned to read the patterns around him. As King David heard the sound of marching in the tops of the balsam trees and knew that the Lord had gone before him to strike down his enemies,[9] so Christ knew

4 Acts 9:1 - 19
5 Genesis 1:26
6 Genesis 3:22
7 Ephesians 4:13
8 Psalm 19:4
9 2 Samuel 5:24

what was happening around him because he knew the pattern. He even takes the religious leaders of his day to task for recognizing physical patterns, but not understanding the spiritual patterns.[10]

If you have ever studied to play an instrument, you know that true mastery lies in learning the pattern of the instrument. This involves a lot of thought and careful repetition. What you are doing is training the body to respond instinctively, and when that happens you begin to discover hidden dimensions in both music and in the instrument.

In the same manner, you need to be trained to respond instinctively in the spirit. Through salvation in Christ you have access to the Spirit of God.[11] The Spirit is the pattern and the pattern maker. Your understanding of the patterns of God come through none but the Spirit of God. This isn't a mental exercise, it is a spiritual exercise.

I was once taught contour drawing. Contour drawing involves placing lines while studying the model, looking at the paper only minimally. The purpose is to train your eye to see what you are looking at while you draw. At the end of one session I was examining my drawing, quite proud of the result, when the instructor walked up to my neighbour and began commenting on his drawing. As I looked at his work, I suddenly *got it.* While my drawing had done a better job of reproducing the surface of the model, his drawing had captured her essence. It was my seminal artistic eureka moment, and has done more to change my relationship with art than any other exercise or teacher or event.

When the pattern of God begins to form in your spiritual self, you will one day wake up and realize that you are experiencing and understanding God in a way that is totally new to you. It is not that God has changed, but rather that previous areas of ignorance in your knowledge of him have been enlightened. Christ speaks of deception

10 Matthew 16:1 - 4
11 John 14:26

that, if possible, threatens even his elect.[12] Deception's favorite target is ignorance. The best way to avoid deception is learning to recognize God.

We are told not to jump to conclusions — a warning against a very human tendency for haste. Yet sometimes it seems as if a jump is the only way to reach a conclusion, especially when it is the things of God that are being discussed. The arguments point to an end, they do not reach an end. Many say that a leap of faith is necessary. Rather, I believe there is a key, a kind of turning we spoke of earlier, which brings recognition of the spiritual.

The scriptures declare that the Kingdom is not in word, but in power.[13] This power is the voice of God. The word goes out void, but it does not return void.[14] At some point that word is given voice — it is empowered. In the beginning the word of God went out, and now that word for this age is being given voice.

The word declares, "Follow me."[15] But every error taught by men down through the ages declares, "Follow me." Voice gives context; voice commands authority. Christ does not say that his sheep know his words, he says that his sheep know his voice.[16] And voice is a characteristic, a pattern. When you begin to recognize the patterns, you begin to recognize God.

There are many debates about the *spiritual vs. literal meaning* of the scriptures. Perhaps it is better if we say *spiritual vs. natural meaning.* We are told that scripture was written by men who were inspired by the Spirit of God.[17] Is the language of the Spirit of God a human tongue? Christ tells his followers that they must eat his flesh and drink his blood.[18] In the language of God this is a literal passage, because it is a spiritual tongue. Some saw in this a teaching too difficult to accept and left him — these saw

12 Matthew 24:24
13 1 Corinthians 4:20
14 Isaiah 55:11
15 Luke 9:59
16 John 10:4
17 2 Timothy 3:16
18 John 6:52-68

only in the natural; others saw words of eternal life — it was the latter who were learning to see in the spiritual.

None of this is possible without the Holy Spirit speaking to you; however, I appreciate more and more Watchman Nee's observation that the spirit tells the forward man to sit at the front and the reticent man to sit at the back.[19] We are all too familiar with the spirit of man, but our call is to become familiar with the Spirit of God.

Most *God moments* are incidental. Pay attention.

19 Watchman Nee, *A Table in the Wilderness*, Tyndale House Publishers, 1965, 1981, May 11th devotional.

12 twelve

a post-communion world

I am about to do a new thing; now it springs forth — do you not perceive it?[1]

Are we to view the resurrection of Christ through his death, or the death of Christ through his resurrection? Paul says that if Christ is not risen from the dead then we are of all men most to be pitied.[2] It is the resurrection that puts the proper perspective on his death.

Remember that Mary Magdalene is representative of the bride of Christ. After two days, Mary Magdalene came to the tomb of Christ but could not find his body.[3] For two thousand years we've known where the body is, but change is now upon us, and the body isn't where it has

1 Isaiah 43:19
2 1 Corinthians 15:12 - 19
3 John 20:1 - 18

always been. And, as was said in the introduction, the difficulty isn't in seeing, it is in recognition. The scriptures say of Mary that, "she turned around and saw Jesus standing there, but she did not know that it was Jesus."[4] The problem wasn't with sight, it was with recognition. Then Jesus spoke her name, and she turned again and beheld the risen Lord.

When Christ asked the Father to, "glorify your name," a voice came from heaven.[5] Some said it was thunder. Others said it was an angel that had spoken. Only one who knew the pattern could hear and understand the voice of God. If you are of the bride, the voice of God will call your name. And you can keep looking around for where the body has been laid, or you can turn and recognize the power of the resurrection.

In the fourth chapter we saw that the time of the Kingdom was described as a time when the first things pass away.[6] This pinpoints the difficulty we will have in the transition. The flesh believes that all things continue as they have since the beginning.[7] But, on that day the peg that was fastened in a secure place will be cut down and fall, and the load that was on it will perish.[8] The way stations we have rested in for thousands of years will be gone.

Another way to look at this is to ask the question, "Was Joshua superior to Moses?" Most of us would put Moses at the head of the list of the heroes of faith. Yet it was Joshua who entered the promise. Don't expect that the institutions and traditions that have served us in the past will carry us into the future, regardless of how excellent they have been. Joshua was called to secure the inheritance of the people of God among and out of seven nations,[9] and it is again the call of God this day to secure the inheritance of his people among and out of seven.

4 John 20:14
5 John 12:27-29
6 Revelation 21:4
7 2 Peter 3:4
8 Isaiah 22:25
9 Joshua 3:10

My grandfather, Carl Nordin, left Sweden and journeyed to America, and then to Canada. He was called to minister to the Scandinavian speaking people of the West. When he came to the end of his life, there were few left who did not speak English, therefore his calling died with him. Did that then invalidate his call? God forbid! Yet why do we mistake completion for invalidation? Many invalidate the Old Testament because of the New. Foolish. And just because the institutions and traditions of the past are drawing to a close does not invalidate them, either. As Christ said, "I came not to destroy the law, but to fulfill it."[10] He comes now not to destroy righteousness, but to fulfill it.

Jean Baudrillard writes, "...it is from the death of God that religions emerge."[11] Bill Johnson says, "The consciousness of mankind remains fixed on the Christ who died, not on the Christ who lives."[12] Death and life are being separated in this hour. Death, and the religion that springs from death, is passing away.

Jesus tells us that we are not to look for the coming of the Kingdom in things that can be observed, for the Kingdom is within us.[13] The Kingdom is sealed inside you, waiting for the end of restraint. You have died and your life is hidden with Christ in God. When Christ, who is your life, is revealed, then you too shall be revealed.[14] We see this as a global event, but what if it begins with individuals, with *first fruits*? What if there is a company of people to whom the coming age is manifest even now?

God is a God of multiplication, but he is also a God of division. That is shown in the first chapter of Genesis. As the word of God separated night and day,[15] so too he is now separating soul from spirit, joint from marrow.[16] The time

10 Matthew 5:17
11 Jean Baudrillard, translated by Sheila Faria Glaser, *Simulacra and Simulation*, The University of Michigan Press, p. 26.
12 Bill Johnson, *When Heaven Invades Earth*, Treasure House - Destiny Image Publishers, p. 146.
13 Luke 17:20-21
14 Colossians 3:3-4
15 Genesis 1:14
16 Hebrews 4:12

has come for judgment to begin with the household of God.[17] And this is the judgment: that light has come into the world.[18] Light brings sight, and sight brings judgment. Judgment separates, and that separation is preparation for that which comes next, just as is shown in the days of creation. Judgment begins with the coming of the Lord.[19] If judgment also begins with the household of God, he then must first come to the household of God. This is a time of the disclosing of things hidden, and it is the eternal which is unseen.[20]

Those of this company will recognize the inheritance implicit in his resurrection, and to them it is as if he has already returned, as if they already inhabit the Kingdom. This is what Christ refers to when he asks if he will find faith on earth when he comes.[21] Faith is imperishable[22] but what is sown, what dies, is perishable,[23] therefore the fullness of faith is not found in death, but in resurrection.

Furthermore, Paul tells us that flesh and blood cannot inherit the Kingdom.[24] The Lord's Supper, the Communion, is based upon flesh and blood. "Those who eat my flesh and drink my blood remain [hidden] in me," Jesus declares.[25] Paul tells us that in the eating of this flesh and the drinking of this blood, you proclaim the Lord's death, until he comes.[26] Now, while it is of no value to cease Communion in the hope of recognizing his coming, for those who have seen the promise it is necessary to lay aside that which proclaims death and move forward into those things which proclaim life.

The cry has gone out as it did in the day of Isaiah, "Whom shall I send, and who will go for us?"[27] If you

17 1 Peter 4:17
18 John 3:19
19 1 Corinthians 4:5
20 2 Corinthians 4:18
21 Luke 18:8
22 1 Corinthians 13:13
23 1 Corinthians 15:42
24 1 Corinthians 15:50
25 John 6:56
26 1 Corinthians 11:26
27 Isaiah 6:8

can no longer find God where you have in the past, and are wandering in what seems a fruitless search for his presence, then I say, "Look up, for your redemption is at hand!"[28] The Lord is calling your name.

The Spirit and the Bride say, "Come."[29]

28 Luke 21:28
29 Revelation 22:17

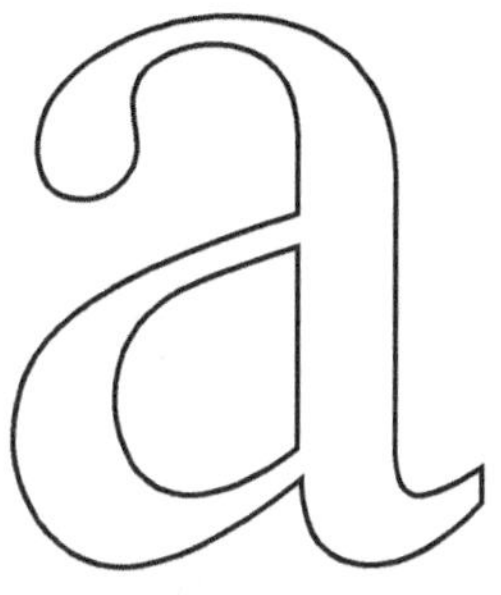

appendix

A good way to wrestle with the braided themes of pattern is to lay out the information in a systematic manner. On the following pages the examples used in the book, plus a couple extras, are arranged step by step.

Examine each step independently. Check the:

pattern of foundation

(2:2:2:1 by grouping 1&2; 3&4; 5&6; 7)

pattern of revelation

(4:2:1 by grouping 1,2,3&4; 5&6; 7).

Look at the center (4).

What do you see?

As an additional exercise, think about the way the two scripture references from the topic of *Mountain* in Chapter 9 are divided. Apply these divisions to the *pattern of revelation* data set (it is often best to begin with the days of creation).

Sets of Seven

Days of Creation	Genesis 1:1 - 2:4
History	
Leah's Children	Genesis 29:32 - 35;30:17 - 21
Revelation's Godhead	*Revelation 1:4*
The Seven Spirits of God	Isaiah 11:2
The Seven Seals	*Revelation 6:1 - 8:5*
New Heaven and Earth	Revelation 21:3 - 4
Wisdom	*Proverbs 9:1 - 3*
Walking (Eden: God walks with man)	Genesis 3:8 - 10; 5:22; 6:9; 17:1; John 14:3
Christ discloses the mystery of God	*1 Timothy 3:16*
The Old Covenant	Hebrews 12:18 - 19
The New Covenant	*Hebrews 12:22 - 24*
David's Song for Victory	Psalm 108:8 - 9
Gabriel's Declaration to Daniel	*Daniel 9:24*
Solomon's Call to Restoration	2 Chronicles 7:14
Sing to the Lord a New Song	*Psalm 96:7 - 10*
Nations' Cry in the Last Days	Micah 4:2 - 3
Seven Trumpets	*Revelation 8:6 - 11:19*
Isaiah's Exodus	Isaiah 52:11 - 12

appendix

One

Day 1	light separated from darkness; day and night
1st thousand years	*Adam to Noah*
Reuben	See, a Son
He Who is	
Fear of the Lord	
1st horseman (white)	*has a bow; given a crown; conquering and to conquer*

The tabernacle of God is among men

Built her house

Man walks with God

Great is the mystery of godliness

A mountain that can be touched

The sprinkled blood, speaking a word better than Abel

Gilead is mine

Seventy sevens are decreed for your people and your holy city

Humble themselves

Give to the Lord, O families of the people

Come, and let us go up to the mountain of the Lord

... 1/3 of the earth is burned up ...

Depart, depart, go out from there

Two

Day 2	waters below firmament separated from water above
2nd thousand years	*Noah to Abraham*
Simeon	One who hears
He Who was	
Knowledge	
2nd horseman (red)	*granted to take peace, men slay one another; given a great sword*

He will tabernacle with them

Hewn her seven pillars

Man walks with God

He was manifest in the flesh

A blazing fire

Jesus, mediator of a better covenant

Manasseh is mine

To finish the transgression

Pray

Give unto the Lord glory and strength

And to the house of the God of Jacob

… 1/3 of the sea becomes blood …

Touch nothing unclean

appendix

Three

Day 3 waters gathered into seas; dry land (earth); vegetation: plants and fruit

3rd thousand years *Abraham to David*

Levi Attached

He Who is to come

Might

3rd horseman (black) *has scales;*
1 qt. wheat for a denarius
and 3 qts. barley for a denarius;
don't harm the oil and wine

They will be his people

Slaughtered her beasts

Man walks before God

Justified by the Spirit

A blackness

Spirits of righteous men made perfect

Ephraim is my helmet

To put an end to sin

Seek my face

Give unto the Lord the glory due his name

That he may teach us his ways

… 1/3 of the sea creatures die …

Go out of the midst of her

Four

center — fulfillment of one

Day 4 lights in the heavens: greater governs the day;
lesser governs the night; stars

4th thousand years *David to Christ*

Judah Praise

The seven Spirits around the throne

Counsel

4th horseman (sickly pale) *has the name of Death;*
Hades follows;
given authority to kill with sword,
famine, pestilence and wild beasts

God himself will be with them and be their God

Mixed her wine

Man walks before God

Seen by angels

Darkness

God, the Judge of all

Judah is my scepter

To atone for iniquity

Turn from their wicked ways

Bring an offering and come into his courts

That we may walk in his paths

… 1/3 of the sun, moon, and stars are darkened …

Purify yourselves, you who carry the vessels of the Lord

appendix

Five

Day 5 — sea creatures; birds

5th thousand years — *Church*

Issachar — Reward

Faithful witness

Understanding

1st judgement — *slain ask "How long?" given white robes and told to rest until all servants and brothers are killed*

He will wipe every tear from their eyes

Set her table

God walks before man

Proclaimed among Gentiles

A tempest

The Church of the firstborn enrolled in heaven

Moab is my washbasin

To bring in everlasting righteousness

I will hear from heaven

Worship the Lord in the beauty of holiness

For the law will go forth from Zion

I saw a star from heaven which had fallen to earth … — *1st woe*

But you will not go out in haste or in flight

Six

Day 6 earth creatures;
man in our image to rule over all creatures

6th thousand years *Church*

Zebulun Honour

Firstborn from the dead

Wisdom

2nd judgement *earthquake; sun black; moon blood;*
stars fall; sky split; mountains and islands moved;
everyone hiding …

Death, mourning, crying and pain will be no more

Sent out her servant girls

God walks before man

Believed in throughout the world

The sound of a trumpet

Innumerable angels in festal assembly

Upon Edom I cast my shoe

To seal both vision and prophet

I will forgive their sin

Fear him all the earth

And the word of the Lord from Jerusalem

… 4 angels bound at the Euphrates are released … *2nd woe*

For the Lord will go before you

Seven

Day 7 | God rests

7th thousand years | *Millennial reign*

Dinah | Justice

Ruler of the Kings of the earth

The Spirit of the Lord

silence in heaven | *incense of prayers thrown to earth; thunder, lightning, earthquake*

For the first things have passed away

Calls from the highest places in the town

?

Taken up in glory

The voice of words

Mount Zion, the city of God, the Heavenly Jerusalem

Over Philistia I shout in triumph

To anoint a most holy one

I will heal their land

Say among the nations, "The Lord reigns"

And he will judge between many peoples

... The kingdom of the world has become the kingdom of our Lord and his Messiah ... | *3rd woe*

And the God of Israel will be your rear guard

About the Author

Tim Nordin and his wife, Carolyn, live in Alberta, Canada. They watch over a flock of sheep, as well as six english sparrows, four dogs, two llamas, two cockatiels and a goose.

www.ingramcontent.com/pod-product-compliance
Lightning Source LLC
LaVergne TN
LVHW091156080426
835509LV00006B/710